KT-223-382

THE PRINCE

Niccolò Machiavelli

COLLINS
CLASSICS

Harper Press
An imprint of HarperCollins*Publishers*
77–85 Fulham Palace Road
Hammersmith
London W6 8JB

This edition published 2011

A catalogue record for this book is available from the British Library

ISBN-13: 978-0-00-742007-0

Printed and bound in Great Britain by Clays Ltd, St Ives plc

Mixed Sources
Product group from well-managed
forests and other controlled sources
www.fsc.org Cert no. SW-COC-001806
© 1996 Forest Stewardship Council

FSC is a non-profit international organisation established to promote the
responsible management of the world's forests. Products carrying the FSC
label are independently certified to assure consumers that they come
from forests that are managed to meet the social, economic and
ecological needs of present and future generations.

Find out more about HarperCollins and the environment at
www.harpercollins.co.uk/green

Translated by William K. Marriott
Life & Times section by Gerard Cheshire
Classic Literature: Words and Phrases adapted from
Collins English Dictionary

Typesetting in Kalix by Palimpsest Book Production Limited,
Falkirk, Stirlingshire

History of Collins

In 1819, millworker William Collins from Glasgow, Scotland, set up a company for printing and publishing pamphlets, sermons, hymn books and prayer books. That company was Collins and was to mark the birth of HarperCollins Publishers as we know it today. The long tradition of Collins dictionary publishing can be traced back to the first dictionary William published in 1824, *Greek and English Lexicon*. Indeed, from 1840 onwards, he began to produce illustrated dictionaries and even obtained a licence to print and publish the Bible.

Soon after, William published the first Collins novel, *Ready Reckoner*, however it was the time of the Long Depression, where harvests were poor, prices were high, potato crops had failed and violence was erupting in Europe. As a result, many factories across the country were forced to close down and William chose to retire in 1846, partly due to the hardships he was facing.

Aged 30, William's son, William II took over the business. A keen humanitarian with a warm heart and a generous spirit, William II was truly 'Victorian' in his outlook. He introduced new, up-to-date steam presses and published affordable editions of Shakespeare's works and *Pilgrim's Progress*, making them available to the masses for the first time. A new demand for educational books meant that success came with the publication of travel books, scientific books, encyclopaedias and dictionaries. This demand to be educated led to the later publication of atlases and Collins also held the monopoly on scripture writing at the time.

In the 1860s Collins began to expand and diversify and the idea of 'books for the millions' was developed. Affordable editions of classical literature were published and in 1903 Collins introduced 10 titles in their Collins Handy Illustrated Pocket Novels. These proved so popular that a few years later this had increased to an output of 50 volumes, selling nearly half a million in their year of publication. In the same year, The Everyman's Library was also instituted, with the idea of publishing an affordable library of the most important classical works, biographies, religious and philosophical treatments, plays, poems, travel and adventure. This series eclipsed all competition at the time and the introduction of paperback books in the 1950s helped to open that market and marked a high point in the industry.

HarperCollins is and has always been a champion of the classics and the current Collins Classics series follows in this tradition – publishing classical literature that is affordable and available to all. Beautifully packaged, highly collectible and intended to be reread and enjoyed at every opportunity.

Life & Times

About the Author

The term 'Machiavellian' is fairly well known in English and other European languages in describing people who manipulate others and circumstances for their own ends. The reason why the word was adopted and is still used is because it conveniently encapsulates any number of pejorative adjectives into a single term, such as scheming, cunning, unscrupulous, amoral, duplicitous, deceitful and unethical. In short: someone who is dishonorable – a scoundrel, a cad or a bounder.

Niccolò Machiavelli, to whom the term alludes, was a political theorist rather than a novelist. He lived in Italy at the turn of the 15th and 16th centuries during the Renaissance period and was a contemporary of another great thinker, Leonardo da Vinci. At that time Italy was not a single nation and Machiavelli was a civil servant for those who ruled the Florentine Republic in the northwest. This city-state was in a perpetual state of political unrest, resulting in feuds and coups between factions of the ruling elite. Machiavelli used his intellect as a means of theorizing how a prince might ensure long-term political control and power in such a turbulent region.

So it was that Machiavelli wrote his treatise, now known as *The Prince*, in an effort to show that politics might be thought of as a science. His notion was fundamentally a simple one; that through careful consideration of actions and reactions it should be possible to manipulate circumstances to ensure a continuance of rule. At a time where the idea of planning ahead and analyzing situations was not commonplace, Machiavelli's approach was nothing short of revolutionary. In effect he had single-handedly invented the science of politics and his book became the blueprint for political strategy from that day forward.

The Machiavellian Treatise

The Prince, which was originally titled *About Principalities*, features an aspiring prince considering various different political strategies in an effort to gain and maintain political stability and so ensure that his reign is lengthy and uninterrupted. By today's standards the book has far less impact, because we know that politicians, as a matter of course, engineer events and circumstances to win votes, but 16th-century Europe was more politically naïve. Machiavelli's book was a little like uncovering the secrets behind a magician's performance and realizing for the first time that illusion and trickery lie behind the façade.

The Prince was virtually a step-by-step book of devious instruction for all politicians. It asserted that there was no place for sincerity and honesty in politics if an individual expected to succeed and make a name for himself. Career politicians needed to be mindful and tactical in all that they said and did. *The Prince* basically gave license to underhand dealing, economy of truth, treachery and spuriousness as part of the political game. No wonder, the term 'Machiavellian' took its place in the lexicons of Europe.

In its favour, *The Prince* is undoubtedly an intelligent and masterful treatise in its entirety. It shows how a willful individual can initially procure or acquire power and then increase and expand on that power. At the same time it denounces poor decision making to ensure that power is never lost and political instability is avoided, and includes advice on how to prevent others with ambition from mustering in on leadership. Consequently, today the book is seen as a kind of exemplar to deliberation on different levels, whether one seeks to hold power within a family, a social group, a company, a political party or a government. According to Machiavelli, power rests on maintaining effective communications and relationships between different parties. It is the implementation of diplomacy, flattery and bribery, sprinkled with charisma and charm, that enables the individual to ensconce himself in a position of lasting power and control.

The crux of Machiavelli's thinking that many people fail to acknowledge upon reading the book is that he is readily describing the very essence and nature of powerful people. Moreover, the truth is that *all* of humanity is Machiavellian to one extent or another and that it is a necessity to have some Machiavellian traits in order to survive in society. If individuals were to speak their minds and do exactly as they pleased then anarchy would likely reign and chaos would ensue. Being 'Machiavellian' is a necessary part of being a social animal, of being human, because we all fit into a hierarchy and we all benefit from the relative respect and power that comes from being good at fitting in and utilizing our social skills. To be devoid of Machiavellian traits entirely would render a person marginalized and impotent.

Machiavelli's book is therefore nothing short of an exposé on the discreditable truth about humanity. In that light, it might even be argued that *The Prince* is an early work of social anthropology as it brings into question whether any behaviour can be viewed as genuinely altruistic. In which case, every aspect of human nature has a Machiavellian undercurrent, no matter how seemingly innocuous or benign. It is a philosophical theme that has been, and will continue to be, debated over and over.

THE PRINCE

CONTENTS

Niccolò Machiavelli to the Most Illustrious
    Lorenzo, Son of Piero De' Medici...................... 1

Chapter 1 The several sorts of Governments,
              and after what manner they are
              obtained 3

Chapter 2 Of Hereditary Principalities..................... 4

Chapter 3 Of Mixed Principalities............................. 6

Chapter 4 Why the Kingdom of Darius,
              usurped by Alexander,
              did not rebel against his Successors,
              after Alexander was dead 16

Chapter 5 How such Cities and Principalities are
              to be governed who lived under
              their own Laws before they were
              subdued 20

Chapter 6 Of Principalities acquired by one's
              own proper conduct and arms........ 22

Chapter 7 Of new Principalities acquired by
              accident and the supplies of other
              people 27

Chapter 8 Of such as have arrived at their

Dominion by wicked and
unjustifiable means...................... 36

Chapter 9 Of Civil Principality 41

Chapter 10 How the strength of all Principalities
is to be computed.......................... 46

Chapter 11 Of Ecclesiastical Principalities 49

Chapter 12 How many Forms there are of
Military Discipline, and of those
Soldiers which are called Mercenary.53

Chapter 13 Of Auxiliaries, Mixed, and Natural
Soldiers.. 60

Chapter 14 The Duty of a Prince in relation
to his Militia................................. 65

Chapter 15 Of such things as render Men
(especially Princes) worthy of Blame
or Applause 69

Chapter 16 Of Liberality and Parsimony................ 71

Chapter 17 Of Cruelty and Clemency, and
whether it is best for a Prince
to be beloved or feared...................74

Chapter 18 How far a Prince is obliged by his
Promise 78

Chapter 19 That Princes ought to be cautious
of becoming either odious or
contemptible.................................. 82

Chapter 20 Whether Citadels, and other things
which Princes many times do,
be profitable or dangerous............ 93

Chapter 21 How a Prince is to demean himself
              to gain reputation 98
Chapter 22 Of the Secretaries of Princes 103
Chapter 23 How Flatterers are to be avoided 105
Chapter 24 How it came to pass that the
              Princes of Italy have most of
              them lost their dominions 108
Chapter 25 How far in human affairs Fortune
              may avail, and in what manner
              she may be resisted 110
Chapter 26 An Exhortation to deliver Italy
              from the Barbarians 114

Niccolò Machiavelli to the Most Illustrious
Lorenzo, Son of Piero De' Medici

Those who desire the favour of a prince do commonly
introduce themselves by presenting him with such things
as he either values much or does more than ordinarily
delight in; for which reason he is frequently presented
with horses, arms, cloth of gold, jewels, and such ornaments as are suitable to his quality and grandeur. Being
ambitious to present myself to your Highness with some
testimony of my devotions towards you, in all my ward-
robe I could not find anything more precious (at least to
myself) than the knowledge of the conduct and achievements of great men, which I learned by long conversation
in modern affairs and a continual investigation of old.
After long and diligent examination, having reduced all
into a small volume, I do presume to present to your
Highness; and though I cannot think it a work fit to
appear in your presence, yet my confidence in your
bounty is such, I hope it may be accepted, considering
I was not capable of more than presenting you with a
faculty of understanding in a short time, what for several
years, with infinite labour and hazard, I had been gath-
ering together. Nor have I beautified or adorned it with
rhetorical ornations, or such outward embellishments as

are usual in such descriptions. I had rather it should pass without any approbation than owe it to anything but the truth and gravity of the matter. I would not have it imputed to me as presumption, if an inferior person, as I am, pretend not only to treat of, but to prescribe and regulate the proceedings of princes; for, as they who take the landscape of a country, to consider the mountains and the nature of the higher places do descend ordinarily into the plains, and dispose themselves upon the hills to take the prospect of the valleys, in like manner, to understand the nature of the people it is necessary to be a prince, and to know the nature of princes it is as requisite to be of the people. May your Highness, then, accept this book with as much kindness as it is presented and if you please diligently and deliberately to reflect upon it you will find in it my extreme desire that your Highness may arrive at that grandeur which fortune and your accomplishments do seem to presage; from which pinnacle of honour, if your Highness vouchsafes at any time to look down upon things below, you will see how unjustly and how continually I have been exposed to the malignity of fortune.

CHAPTER I

The several sorts of Governments, and after what manner they are obtained

There never was nor is at this day any government in the world by which one man has rule and dominion over another, but it is either a commonwealth, or a monarchy. Monarchies are either hereditary, where the ancestors of the sovereign have been a long time in possession, or where they are but new. The new are either so wholly and entirely (as Milan was to Francis Sforza), or annexed to the hereditary dominions of the conqueror (as the kingdom of Naples to the kingdom of Spain). These territories thus acquired are accustomed either to be subject to some prince, or to live at liberty and free, and are subdued either by his auxiliaries or own forces, by his good fortune or conduct.

CHAPTER 2

Of Hereditary Principalities

I shall omit speaking of commonwealths, as having discoursed of them largely elsewhere, and write in this place only of principalities, and how, according to the foregoing division, the said principalities may be governed and maintained. I do affirm, then, that hereditary states, and such as have been accustomed to the family of their prince, are preserved with less difficulty than the new, and because it is sufficient not to transgress the examples of their predecessors, and next to comply and frame themselves to the accidents that occur. So that, if the prince be a person of competent industry, he will be sure to keep himself in the throne, unless he be supplanted by some great and more than ordinary force; and even then, when so supplanted, fortune can never turn tail, or be adverse to the usurper, but he will stand fair to be restored. Of this Italy affords us an example in the Duke of Ferrara, who supported bravely against the invasion of the Venetians in 1484, and afterwards against Pope Julius X, upon no other foundation but his antiquity in that government; for a natural prince has not so much occasion or necessity to oppress his subjects, whereby it follows he must be better beloved, and retain more of the affections of his people, unless some extraordinary vices concur to make him odious; so that the succession and coherence of his government takes away the causes and memory of innovations; for one new change leaves always (as in buildings) a toothing and aptitude of another.

CHAPTER 3

Of Mixed Principalities

But the difficulties consist in governments lately acquired, especially if not absolutely new, but as members annexed to the territories of the usurper, in which case such a government is called mixed. The tumults and revolutions in such monarchies proceed from a natural crossness and difficulty in all new conquests; for men do easily part with their prince upon hopes of bettering their condition, and that hope provokes them to rebel; but most commonly they are mistaken, and experience tells them their condition is much worse.

This proceeds from another natural and ordinary cause, necessitating the new prince to overlay or disgust his new subjects by quartering his army upon them, taxes, or a thousand other inconveniences, which are the perpetual consequents of conquest. So that you make them your enemies who suffer, and are injured by your usurpation, but cannot preserve their friendship who introduced you, because you are neither able to satisfy their expectation, or employ strong remedies against them, by reason of your obligations; wherefore, though an usurper be never so strong, and his army never so numerous, he must have intelligence with the natives if he means to conquer a province. For these reasons Louis

XII of France quickly subdued Milan, and lost it as quickly; for the same people which opened him their gates, finding themselves deceived in their hopes, and disappointed in the future benefits which they expected, could not brook nor comport with the haughtiness of their new sovereign: it is very true countries that have rebelled and are conquered the second time are recovered with more difficulty; for the defection of the people having taken off all obligation or respect from the usurper, he takes more liberty to secure himself by punishing offenders, exposing the suspected, and fortifying wherever he finds himself weak; so that Count Lodovick having been able to rescue Milan out of the hands of the French the first time only by harassing and infesting its borders, the second time he recovered it it was necessary for him to arm and confederate the whole world against the said king, and that his army should be beaten and driven out of Italy; and this happened from the aforesaid occasions: nevertheless the French were twice dispossessed. The general reasons of the first we have already discoursed, it remains now that we take a prospect of the second, and declare what remedies the said King Louis had, or what another may have in his condition, to preserve himself better in his new conquests than the King of France did before him. I say, then, that provinces newly acquired, and joined to the ancient territory of him who conquered them, are either of the same country, or language, or otherwise. In the first case they are easily kept, especially if the people have not been too much accustomed to liberty; and to secure the possession there needs no more than to extirpate the family of the prince which governed before; for in other things maintaining to them their old condition, there being no discrepancy in their customs, men do acquiesce and live quietly, as has been seen in the cases of Burgundy, Bretagne,

Gascoigne, and Normandy, which have continued so long under the government of France; for though there be some difference in their language, nevertheless, their laws and customs being alike, they do easily consist. He therefore who acquires anything, and desires to preserve it, is obliged to have a care of two things more particularly; one is, that the family of the former prince be extinguished; the other, that no law or taxes be imposed: whereby it will come to pass, that in a short time it may be annexed and consolidated with his old principality. But where conquest is made in a country differing in language, customs and laws, there is the great difficulty; their good fortune and great industry is requisite to keep it. And one of the best and most efficacious expedients to do it would be for the usurper to live there himself, which would render his possession more secure and durable, as the great Turk has done in Greece, who, in despite of all his practices and policies to keep it in subjection, had he not fixed his imperial residence there would never have been able to have effected it. For being present in person, disorders are discovered in the bud and prevented, but being at a distance in some remote part, they come only by hearsay, and that, when they are got to a head, are commonly incurable. Besides, the province is not subject to be pillaged by officers, by reason of the nearness and accessibleness of their prince, which disposes those to love him who are good, and those to dread him who are otherwise; and if any foreigner attacks it, he must do it with more care and circumspection, in respect that the prince's residence being there it will be harder for him to lose it.

There is another remedy, rather better than worse, and that is, to plant colonies in one or two places, which may be as it were the keys of that State, and either that must be done of necessity, or an army of horse and foot be maintained in those parts, which is much worse; for colonies are of no great expense; the Prince sends and maintains them at very little charge, and intrenches only upon such as he is constrained to dispossess of their houses and land for the subsistence and accommodation of the new inhabitants, who are but few, and a small part of the State; they also who are injured and offended, living dispersed and in poverty, cannot do any mischief, and the rest being quiet and undisturbed, will not stir, lest they should mistake and run themselves into the same condition with their neighbours.

I conclude, likewise, that those colonies which are least chargeable are most faithful and inoffensive, and those few who are offended are too poor and dispersed to do any hurt, as I said before; and it is to be observed, men are either to be flattered and indulged or utterly destroyed—because for small offences they do usually revenge themselves, but for great ones they cannot—so that injury is to be done in such a manner as not to fear any revenge. But if instead of colonies an army be kept on foot, it will be much more expensive, and the whole revenue of that province being consumed in the keeping it, the acquisition will be a loss, and rather a prejudice than otherwise, by removing the camp up and down the country, and changing their quarters, which is an inconvenience every man will resent and be ready to revenge, and they are the most dangerous and implacable enemies who are provoked by insolences committed against them in their own houses. In all respects, therefore, this kind of guard is unprofitable, whereas on the other side colonies are useful. Moreover, he who is in a province of a different constitution, as is said before, ought to make himself head and protector of his inferior neighbours, and endeavour with all diligence to weaken and debilitate such as are more powerful, and to have a particular care that no stranger enters into the said province with as much power as he; for it will always happen that somebody or other will be invited by the malcontents, either out of ambition or fear. This is visible in the Etolians, who brought the Romans into Greece, who were never admitted into any province but by the temptation of the natives. The common method in such cases is this: as soon as a foreign potentate enters into a province, those who are weaker or disobliged join themselves with him out of emulation and animosity to those who are above them, insomuch that in respect of these inferior lords, no pains is to be omitted that may gain them; and when gained, they will readily and unanimously fall into one mass with the State that is conquered. Only the conqueror is to take special care they grow not too strong, nor be entrusted with too much authority, and then he can easily with his own forces and their assistance keep down the greatness of his neighbours, and make himself absolute arbiter in that province. And he who acts not this part prudently shall quickly lose what he has got, and even whilst he enjoys it be obnoxious to many troubles and inconveniences. The Romans in their new conquests observed this course, they planted their colonies, entertained the inferior lords into their protection without increasing their power; they kept under such as were more potent, and would not suffer any foreign prince to have interest among them. I will set down only Greece for an example. The Etolians and Achaians were protected, the kingdom of the Macedonians was depressed and Antiochus driven out; yet the merits and fidelity of the Achaians and Etolians could never procure them any increase of authority, nor the persuasions and applications of Philip induce the Romans to be his friends till he was overcome, nor the power of Antiochus prevail with them to consent that he should retain any sovereignty in that province: for the Romans acted in that case as all wise princes ought to do who are to have an eye not only upon present but future incommodities, and to redress them with all possible industry; for dangers that are seen afar off are easily prevented, but protracting till they are at hand, the remedies grow unseasonable and the malady incurable. And it falls out in this case, as the physicians say of an hectic fever, that at first it is easily cured and hard to be known, but in process of time, not being observed or resisted in the beginning, it becomes easy to be known but very difficult to be cured. So it is in matters of state, things which are discovered at a distance—which is done only by prudent men—produce little mischief but what is easily averted; but when through ignorance or inadvertency they come to that height that every one discerns them, there is no room for any remedy, and the disease is incurable. The Romans, therefore, foreseeing their troubles afar off, opposed themselves in time, and never swallowed any injury to put off a war, for they knew that war was not avoided but deferred thereby, and commonly with advantage to the enemy; wherefore they chose rather to make war upon Philip, and Antiochus in Greece, than suffer them to invade Italy; and yet at that time there was no necessity of either; they might have avoided them both, but they thought it not fit; for they could never relish the saying that is so frequent in the mouths of our new politicians "to enjoy the present benefit of time," but preferred the exercise of their courage and wisdom, for time carries all things along with it, and may bring good as well as evil, and ill as well as good. But let us return to France, and examine if what was there done was conformable to what is prescribed here; and to this purpose I shall not speak of Charles VIII but of Louis XII, as of a prince whose conduct and affairs (by reason his possession was longer in Italy) were more conspicuous, and you shall see how contrary he acted in everything that was necessary for the keeping of so different a State. This Louis was invited into Italy by the Venetians, who had an ambition to have got half Lombardy by his coming. I will not condemn the expedition, nor blame the counsels of that King for being desirous of footing in Italy, and having no allies left in that country, but all doors shut against him (upon the ill-treatment which his predecessor Charles had used towards them) he was constrained to take his friends where he could find them, and that resolution would have been lucky enough had he not miscarried in his other administration; for he had no sooner subdued Lombardy but he recovered all the reputation and dignity that was lost by King Charles. Genoa submitted, Florence courted his friendship, the Marquis of Mantua, the Duke of Ferrara, Bentivoglio, Madam de Furli, the Lords of Faenza, Pesoro, Rimini, Camerino, Piombino; the Lucchesi, Pisani, Sanesi, all of them address themselves to him for his alliance and amity; then the Venetians began to consider and reflect upon their indiscretion, who, to gain two towns in Lombardy, had made the King of France master of two-thirds of all Italy. Let any one now think with how little difficulty the said king might have kept up his reputation in that country if he had observed the rules aforesaid and protected his friends, who being numerous, and yet weak and fearful (some of the Pope, and some of the Venetians), were always under a necessity of standing by him, and with their assistance he might easily have secured himself against any competitor whatever. But he was no sooner in Milan but he began to prevaricate and send supplies to Pope Alexander to put him in possession of Romagna, not considering that thereby he weakened himself and disobliged his friends who had thrown themselves into his arms, and aggrandized the Church by adding to its spiritual authority (which was so formidable before) so great a proportion of temporal; and having committed one error, he was forced to proceed so far as to put a stop to the ambition of Pope Alexander, and hinder his making himself master of Tuscany; the said Louis was forced into Italy again. Nor was it enough for him to have advanced the interest of the Church and deserted his friends, but out of an ardent desire to the kingdom of Naples he shared it with the King of Spain; so that whereas before he was sole umpire in Italy, he now entertained a partner, to whom the ambitious of that province and his own malcontents might repair upon occasion; and whereas the King of that kingdom might have been made his pensioner, he turned out him to put in another that might be able to turn out himIt is very obvious, and no more than natural, for princes to desire to extend their dominion, and when they attempt nothing but what they are able to achieve they are applauded, at least not upbraided thereby; but when they are unable to compass it, and yet will be doing, then they are condemned, and indeed not unworthily.

If France, then, with its own forces alone, had been able to have enterprised upon Naples, it ought to have been done; but if her own private strength was too weak, it ought not to have been divided: and if the division of Lombardy, to which he consented with the Venetian, was excusable, it was because done to get footing in Italy; but this partition of Naples with the King of Spain is extremely to be condemned, because not pressed or quickened by such necessity as the former. Louis therefore committed five faults in this expedition. He ruined the inferior lords; he augmented the dominion of a neighbour prince; he called in a foreigner as puissant as himself; he neglected to continue there in person; and planted no colonies—all which errors might have been no inconvenience whilst he had lived, had he not been guilty of a sixth, and that was depressing the power of the Venetian. If indeed he had not sided with the Church, nor brought the Spaniards into Italy, it had been but reasonable for him to have taken down the pride of the Venetian; but pursuing his first resolutions, he ought not to have suffered them to be ruined, because whilst the Venetian strength was entire, they would have kept off other people from attempting upon Lombardy, to which the Venetian would never have consented, unless upon condition it might have been delivered to them, and the others would not in probability have forced it from France to have given it to them; and to have contended with them both nobody would have had the courage. If it be urged that King Louis gave up Romagna to the Pope, and the kingdom of Naples to the King of Spain, to evade a war, I answer, as before, that a present mischief is not to be suffered to prevent a war, for the war is not averted but protracted, and will follow with greater disadvantage.

If the King's faith and engagements to the Pope to undertake this enterprise for him be objected, and that he did it to recompense the dissolution of his marriage, and the cap which at his intercession his Holiness had conferred upon the Legate of Amboise, I refer them for an answer to what I shall say hereafter about the faith of a prince, how far it obliges. So then King Louis lost Lombardy because he did not observe one of those rules which others have followed with success in the conquest of provinces, and in their desire to keep them; nor is it an extraordinary thing, but what happens every day, and not without reason. To this purpose, I remember I was once in discourse with the Cardinal d'Amboise at Nantes, at the time when Valentino (for so Cæsar Borgia, Pope

Alexander's son was commonly called) possessed himself of Romagna. In the heat of our conference, the Cardinal telling me that the Italians were ignorant of the art of war, I replied that the French had as little skill in matters of State; for if they had had the least policy in the world they would never have suffered the Church to have come to that height and elevation. And it has been found since by experience, that the grandeur of the Church and the Spaniard in Italy is derived from France, and that they in requital have been the ruin and expulsion of the French.

From hence a general rule may be deduced, and such a one as seldom or never is subject to exception,—viz., that whoever is the occasion of another's advancement is the cause of his own diminution; because that advancement is founded either upon the conduct or power of the donor, either of which become suspicious at length to the person preferred.

CHAPTER 4

Why the Kingdom of Darius, usurped by
Alexander, did not rebel against his
Successors, after Alexander was dead

The difficulties encountered in the keeping of a new
conquest being considered, it may well be admired how
it came to pass that Alexander the Great, having in a
few years made himself master of Asia, and died as soon
as he had done, that State could be kept from rebellion;
yet his successors enjoyed it a long time peaceably
without any troubles or concussions but what sprung
from their own avarice and ambition. I answer that all
monarchies of which we have any record were governed
after two several manners; either by a prince and his
servants whom he vouchsafes out of his mere grace to
constitute his ministers, and admits of their assistance
in the government of his kingdom; or else by a prince
and his barons, who were persons advanced to that
quality, not by favour or concession of the prince, but
by the ancientness and nobility of their extraction. These
barons have their proper jurisdictions and subjects, who
own their authority and pay them a natural respect.
Those States which are governed by the prince and his
servants have their prince more arbitrary and absolute,

because his supremacy is acknowledged by everybody; and if another be obeyed, it is only as his minister and substitute, without any affection to the man. Examples of these different governments we may find in our time in the persons of the Grand Signor and the King of France. The whole Turkish monarchy is governed by a single person, the rest are but his servants and slaves; for distinguishing his whole monarchy into provinces and governments (which they call Sangiacchi) he sends when and what officers he thinks fit, and changes them as he pleases. But the King of France is established in the middle, as it were, of several great lords, whose sovereignty having been owned, and families beloved a long time by their subjects, they keep their pre-eminence; nor is it in the king's power to deprive them without inevitable danger to himself. He, therefore, who considers the one with the other will find the Turkish empire harder to be subdued; but when once conquered more easy to be kept. The reason of the difficulty is, because the usurper cannot be called in by the grandees of the empire, nor hope any assistance from the great officers to facilitate his enterprise, which proceeds from the reasons aforesaid; for being all slaves and under obligation they are not easily corrupted; and if they could, little good was to be expected from them, being unable for the aforesaid reasons to bring them any party: so that whoever invades the Turk must expect to find him entire and united, and is to depend more upon his own proper force than any disorders among them; but having once conquered them, and beaten their army beyond the possibility of a recruit, the danger is at an end; for there is nobody remaining to be afraid of but the family of the emperor, which, being once extinguished, nobody else has any interest with the people, and they are as little to be apprehended after the victory as they were to be relied upon before. But in kingdoms that are governed according to the model of France it happens quite contrary, because having gained some of the barons to your side (and some of them will always be discontented and desirous of change), you may readily enter; they can, as I said before, give you easy admission and contribute to your victory. But to defend and make good what you have got brings a long train of troubles and calamities with it, as well upon your friends as your foes. Nor will it suffice to exterminate the race of the king; forasmuch as other princes will remain, who, upon occasion, will make themselves heads of any commotion, and they being neither to be satisfied nor extinguished, you must of necessity be expelled upon the first insurrection.

Now, if it be considered what was the nature of Darius's government, it will be found to have been very like the Turks, and therefore Alexander was obliged to fight them, and having conquered them, and Darius dying after the victory, the empire of the Persians remained quietly to Alexander, for the reasons aforesaid; and his successors, had they continued united, might have enjoyed it in peace, for in that whole empire no tumults succeeded but what were raised by themselves. But in kingdoms that are constituted like France it is otherwise, and impossible to possess them in quiet. From hence sprung the many defections of Spain, France and Greece from the Romans, by reason of the many little principalities in those several kingdoms of which, whilst there remained any memory, the Romans enjoyed their possession in a great deal of uncertainty; but when their memory was extinct by power and diuturnity of empire, they grew secure in their possessions, and quarrelling afterwards among themselves, every officer of the Romans was able to bring a party into the field, according to the latitude and extent of his command in the said provinces; and the reason was, because the race of their old princes being extirpate, there was nobody left for them to acknowledge but the Romans. These things, therefore, being considered, it is not to be wondered that Alexander had the good fortune to keep the empire of Asia, whilst the rest, as Pyrrhus and others, found such difficulty to retain what they had got; for it came not to pass from the small or great virtue of the victor, but from the difference and variety of the subject.

CHAPTER 5

Sabotage such Cities and Principalities are to
be governed who lived under their own
Laws before they were subdued

When States that are newly conquered have been accustomed to their liberty, and lived under their own laws,
to keep them three ways are to be observed: the first is
utterly to ruin them; the second, to live personally among
them; the third is (contenting yourself with a pension
from them) to permit them to enjoy their old privileges
and laws, erecting a kind of Council of State, to consist
of a few which may have a care of your interest, and
keep the people in amity and obedience. And that
Council being set up by you, and knowing that it subsists
only by your favour and authority, will not omit anything
that may propagate and enlarge them. A town that has
been anciently free cannot more easily be kept in subjection than by employing its own citizens, as may be seen
by the example of the Spartans and Romans. The Spartans
had got possession of Athens and Thebes, and settled an
oligarchy according to their fancy; and yet they lost them
again. The Romans, to keep Capua, Carthage and
Numantia, ordered them to be destroyed, and they kept
them by that means. Thinking afterwards to preserve

Greece, as the Spartans had done, by allowing them their liberty, and indulging their old laws, they found themselves mistaken; so that they were forced to subvert many cities in that province before they could keep it; and certainly that is the safest way which I know; for whoever conquers a free town and does not demolish it commits a great error, and may expect to be ruined himself; because whenever the citizens are disposed to revolt, they betake themselves of course to that blessed name of liberty, and the laws of their ancestors, which no length of time nor kind usage whatever will be able to eradicate; and let all possible care and provision be made to the contrary, unless they be divided some way or other, or the inhabitants dispersed, the thought of their old privileges will never out of their heads, but upon all occasions they will endeavour to recover them, as Pisa did after it had continued so many years in subjection to the Florentines. But it falls out quite contrary where the cities or provinces have been used to a prince whose race is extirpated and gone; for being on the one side accustomed to obey, and on the other at a loss for their old family, they can never agree to set up another, and will never know how to live freely without; so that they are not easily to be tempted to rebel, and the prince may oblige them with less difficulty, and be secure of them when he hath done. But in a commonwealth their hatred is more inveterate, their revenge more insatiable; nor does the memory of their ancient liberty ever suffer, or ever can suffer them to be quiet; so that the most secure way is either to ruin them quite, or make your residence among them.

CHAPTER 6

Of Principalities acquired by one's own proper conduct and arms

Let no man think it strange if in speaking of new governments, either by princes or states, I introduce great and eminent examples; forasmuch as men in their actions follow commonly the ways that are beaten, and when they would do any generous thing they propose to themselves some pattern of that nature; nevertheless, being impossible to come up exactly to that, or to acquire that virtue in perfection which you desire to imitate; a wise man ought always to set before him for his example the actions of great men who have excelled in the achievement of some great exploit, to the end that though his virtue and power arrives not at that perfection, it may at least come as near as is possible, and receive some tincture thereby. Like experienced archers, who observing the mark to be at great distance, and knowing the strength of their bow, and how far it will carry, they fix their aim somewhat higher than the mark, not with design to shoot at that height, but that by mounting their arrow to a certain proportion, they may come the nearer to the mark they intend. I say, then, that principalities newly acquired by an upstart prince are more or less difficult to maintain, as he is more or less provident that gains them. And because the happiness of rising from a private person to be a prince presupposes great virtue or fortune, where both of them concur they do much facilitate the conservation of the conquest; yet he who has committed least to fortune has continued the longest. It prevents much trouble likewise, when the prince (having no better residence elsewhere) is constrained to live personally among them. But to speak of such who by their virtue, rather than fortune, have advanced themselves to that dignity, I say that the most renowned and excellent are Moses, Cyrus, Romulus, Theseus, and the like. And though Moses might be reasonably excepted, as being only the executioner of God's immediate commands, yet he deserves to be mentioned, if it were only for that grace which rendered him capable of communication with God. But if we consider Cyrus, and the rest of the conquerors and founders of monarchies, we shall find them extraordinary; and examining their lives and exploits, they will appear not much different from Moses, who had so incomparable a Master; for by their conversations and successes they do not seem to have received anything from fortune but occasion and opportunity, in introducing what forms of government they pleased; and as without that occasion the greatness of their courage had never been known, so had not they been magnanimous, and taken hold of it, that occasion had happened in vain. It was necessary, therefore, for Moses that the people of Israel should be in captivity in Egypt that to free themselves from bondage they might be disposed to follow him. It was convenient that Romulus should be turned out of Albo, and exposed to the wild beasts when he was young, that he might afterwards be made King of Rome, and founder of that great empire. It was not unnecessary, likewise, that Cyrus should find the Persians mutinying at the tyranny of the Medes, and that the Medes should be grown soft and effeminate with their long peace. Theseus could never have given proof of his virtue and generosity had not the Athenians been in great trouble and confusion. These great advantages made those great persons eminent, and their great wisdom knew how to improve them to the reputation and enlargement of their country. They, then, who become great by the ways of virtue (as the princes aforesaid) do meet with many difficulties before they arrive at their ends, but having compassed them once they easily keep them. The difficulties in the acquisition arise in part from new laws and customs which they are forced to introduce for the establishment and security of their own dominion; and this is to be considered, that there is nothing more difficult to undertake, more uncertain to succeed, and more dangerous to manage, than to make one's self prince, and prescribe new laws. Because he who innovates in that manner has for his enemies all those who made any advantage by the old laws; and those who expect benefit by the new will be but cool and lukewarm in his defence; which lukewarmness proceeds from a certain awe for their adversaries, who have their old laws on their side, and partly from a natural incredulity in mankind, which gives credit but slowly to any new thing, unless recommended first by the experiment of success. Hence it proceeds, that the first time the adversary has opportunity to make an attempt, he does it with great briskness and vigour; but the defence is so trepid and faint, that for the most part the new prince and his adherents perish together. Wherefore for better discussion of this case it is necessary to inquire whether these innovators do stand upon their own feet, or depend upon other people; that is to say whether in the conduct of their affairs they do make more use of their rhetoric than their arms. In the first case they commonly miscarry, and their designs seldom succeed;

but when their expectations are only from themselves, and they have power in their own hands to make themselves obeyed, they run little or no hazard, and do frequently prevail. For further eviction, the Scripture shows us that those of the prophets whose arms were in their hands, and had power to compel, succeeded better in the reformations which they designed; whereas those who came only with exhortation and good language suffered martyrdom and banishment, because (besides the reasons aforesaid) the people are inconstant and susceptible of any new doctrine at first, but not easily brought to retain it; so that things are to be ordered in such manner that when their faith begins to stagger they may be forced to persist. Moses, Cyrus, Theseus, and Romulus could never have made their laws to have been long observed had they not had power to have compelled it; as in our days it happened to Friar Jerome Savonarola, who ruined himself by his new institutions as soon as the people of Florence began to desert him, for he had no means to confirm them who had been of his opinion, nor to constrain such as dissented. Wherefore such persons meet with great difficulty in their affairs; all their dangers are still by the way, which they can hardly overcome, but by some extraordinary virtue and excellence; nevertheless, when once they have surmounted them, and arrived at any degree of veneration, having supplanted those who envied their advancement, they remain puissant and firm, and honourable and happy. I will add to these great examples another, perhaps not so conspicuous, but one that will bear a proportion and resemblance with the rest, and shall satisfy me for all others of that nature. It is of Hiero of Syracuse, who of a private person was made prince of that city, for which he was beholding to fortune no further than for the occasion, because the Syracusans being under oppression chose him for their captain, in which command he behaved himself so well he deserved to be made their prince, for he was a person of so great virtue and excellence that those who have written of him have given him this character, that even in his private condition he wanted nothing but a kingdom to make him an admirable king. This Hiero subdued the old militia, established a new; renounced the old allies, confederated with others, and having friends and forces of his own, he was able upon such a foundation to erect what fabric he pleased, so that though the acquisition cost him much trouble he maintained it with little.

CHAPTER 7

Of new Principalities acquired by accident
and the supplies of other people

They who from private condition ascend to be princes,
and merely by the indulgence of fortune, arrive without
much trouble at their dignity, though it costs them dear
to maintain it, meet but little difficulty in their passage,
being hurried as it were with wings, yet when they come
to settle and establish then begins their misery. These
kind of persons are such as attain their dignity by bribes,
or concession of some other great prince, as it happened
to several in Greece, in the cities of Ionia, and upon the
Hellespont, where they were invested with that power
by Darius for his greater security and glory, and to those
emperors who arrived at the empire by the corruption
of the soldiers. These persons, I say, subsist wholly upon
the pleasure and fortune of those who advanced them,
which being two things very valuable and uncertain,
they have neither knowledge nor power to continue long
in that degree; know not, because, unless he be a man
of extraordinary qualities and virtue, it is not reasonable
to think he can know how to command other people,
who before lived always in a private condition himself;
cannot, because they have no forces upon whose friendship and fidelity they can rely. Moreover, States which

are suddenly conquered (as all things else in Nature whose rise and increase is so speedy) can have no root or foundation but what will be shaken and supplanted by the first gust of adversity, unless they who have been so suddenly exalted be so wise as to prepare prudently in time for the conservation of what fortune threw so luckily into their lap, and establish afterwards such fundamentals for their duration as others (which I mentioned before) have done in the like cases. About the arrival at this authority either by virtue, or good fortune, I shall instance in two examples that are fresh in our memory; one is Francis Sforza, the other Cæsar Borgia; Sforza, by just means and extraordinary virtue, made himself Duke of Milan, and enjoyed it in great peace, though gained with much trouble. Borgia, on the other side (called commonly Duke of Valentine), got several fair territories by the fortune of his father Pope Alexander, and lost them all after his death, though he used all his industry, and employed all the arts which a wise and brave prince ought to do to fix himself in the sphere where the arms and fortune of other people had placed him: for he, as I said before, who laid not his foundation in time, may yet raise his superstructure, but with great trouble to the architect and great danger to the building. If, therefore, the whole progress of the said Duke be considered, it will be found what solid founda-tions he had laid for his future dominion, of which progress I think it not superfluous to discourse, because I know not what better precepts to display before a new prince than the example of his actions; and though his own orders and methods did him no good, it was not so much his fault as the malignity of his fortune.

Pope Alexander the Sixth had a desire to make his son Duke Valentine great, but he saw many blocks and impediments in the way, both for the present and future.

First, he could not see any way to advance him to any territory that depended not upon the Church; and to those in his gift he was sure the Duke of Milan and the Venetians would never consent; for Faenza and Riminum had already put themselves under the Venetian protection. He was likewise sensible that the forces of Italy, especially those who were capable of assisting him, were in the hands of those who ought to apprehend the greatness of the Pope, as the Ursini, Colonnesi, and their followers, and therefore could not repose any great confidence in them; besides, the laws and alliances of all the States in Italy must of necessity be disturbed before he could make himself master of any part, which was no hard matter to do, finding the Venetians, upon some private interest of their own, inviting the French to another expedition into Italy, which his Holiness was so far from opposing that he promoted it by dissolution of King Louis's former marriage. Louis therefore passed the Alps by the assistance of the Venetians and Alexander's consent, and was no sooner in Milan but he sent forces to assist the Pope in his enterprise against Romagna, which was immediately surrendered upon the king's reputation. Romagna being in this manner reduced by the Duke, and the Colonnesi defeated, being ambitious not only to keep what he had got, but to advance in his conquests, two things obstructed: one was the infidelity of his own army, the other the aversion of the French; for he was jealous of the forces of the Ursini who were in his service, suspected they would fail him in his need, and either hinder his conquest or take it from him when he had done; and the same fears he had of the French. And his jealousy of the Ursini was much increased when, after the expugnation of Faenza, assaulting Bologna, he found them very cold and backward in the attack. And the King's inclination he discovered when, having possessed himself of the Duchy of Urbin, he invaded Tuscany, and was by him required to desist. Whereupon the Duke resolved to depend no longer upon fortune and foreign assistance, and the first course he took was to weaken the party of the Ursini and Colonni in Rome, which he effected very neatly by debauching such of their adherents as were gentlemen, taking them into his own service, and giving them honourable pensions and governments and commands, according to their respective qualities; so that in a few months their passion for that faction evaporated, and they turned all for the Duke. After this he attended an opportunity of supplanting the Ursini, as he had done the family of the Colonni before, which happened very luckily, and was as luckily improved: for the Ursini, considering too late that the greatness of the Duke and the Church tended to their ruin, held a council at a place called Magione, in Perugia, which occasioned the rebellion of Urbin, the tumults in Romagna, and a thousand dangers to the Duke besides; but though he overcame them all by the assistance of the French, and recovered his reputation, yet he grew weary of his foreign allies, as having nothing further to oblige them, and betook himself to his artifice, which he managed so dexterously that the Ursini reconciled themselves to him by the mediation of Seignor Paulo, with whom for his security he comported so handsomely by presenting with money, rich stuffs, and horses, that being convinced of his integrity, he conducted them to Sinigaglia, and delivered them into the Duke's hands. Having by this means exterminated the chief of his adversaries, and reduced their friends, the Duke had laid a fair foundation for his greatness, having gained Romagna and the Duchy of Urbin, and insinuated with the people by giving them a gust of their future felicity. And because this part is not unworthy to be known for imitation sake,

I will not pass it in silence. When the Duke had possessed himself of Romagna, finding it had been governed by poor and inferior lords, who had rather robbed than corrected their subjects, and given them more occasion of discord than unity, insomuch as that province was full of robberies, riots, and all manner of insolencies; to reduce them to unanimity and subjection to monarchy, he thought it necessary to provide them a good governor, and thereupon he conferred that charge upon Remiro d'Orco, with absolute power, though he was a cruel and passionate man. Orco was not long before he had settled it in peace, with no small reputation to himself. Afterwards, the Duke, apprehending so large a power might grow odious to the people, he erected a court of judicature in the middle of the province, in which every city had its advocate, and an excellent person was appointed to preside. And because he discovered that his past severity had created him many enemies, to remove that ill opinion, and recover the affections of the people, he had a mind to show that, if any cruelty had been exercised, it proceeded not from him but from the arrogance of his minister; and for their further confirmation, he caused the said governor to be apprehended, and his head chopped off one morning in the marketplace at Cesena, with a wooden dagger on one side of him and a bloody knife on the other; the ferocity of which spectacle not only appeased but amazed the people for a while. But resuming our discourse, I say, the Duke finding himself powerful enough, and secure against present danger, being himself as strong as he desired, and his neighbours in a manner reduced to an incapacity of hurting him, being willing to go on with his conquests, there remaining nothing but a jealousy of France, and not without cause, for he knew that king had found his error at last, and would be sure to obstruct him. Hereupon he began to look abroad for new allies, and to hesitate and stagger towards France, as appeared when the French army advanced into the kingdom of Naples against the Spaniards, who had besieged Cajeta. His great design was to secure himself against the French, and he had doubtless done it if Alexander had lived. These were his provisions against the dangers that were imminent; but those that were remote were more doubtful and uncertain. The first thing he feared was lest the next Pope should be his enemy, and reassume all that Alexander had given him, to prevent which he proposed four several ways. The first was by destroying the whole line of those lords whom he had dispossessed, that his Holiness might have no occasion to restore them. The second was to cajole the nobility in Rome, and draw them over to his party, that thereby he might put an awe and restraint upon the Pope. The third was, if possible, to make the College his friends. The fourth was to make himself so strong before the death of his father as to be able to stand upon his own legs and repel the first violence that should be practised against him. Three of these four expedients he had tried before Alexander died, and was in a fair way for the fourth; all the disseized lords which came into his clutches he put to death, and left few of them remaining; he had insinuated with the nobility of Rome, and got a great party in the College of Cardinals; and as to his own corroboration, he had designed to make himself master of Tuscany, had got possession of Perugia and Piombino already, and taken Pisa into his protection. And having now farther regard of the French (who were beaten out of the kingdom of Naples by the Spaniard, and both of them reduced to necessity of seeking his amity), he leaped bluntly into Pisa, after which Lucca and Sienna submitted without much trouble, partly in hatred to the Florentines, and partly for fear; and the

Florentines were grown desperate and without any hopes of relief; so that had these things happened before, as they did the same year in which Alexander died, doubtless he had gained so much strength and reputation that he would have stood firm by himself upon the basis of his own power and conduct, without depending upon fortune or any foreign supplies. But his father died five years after his son had taken up arms, and left him nothing solid and in certainty, but Romagna only, and the rest were *in nubibus*, infested with two formidable armies, and himself mortally sick. This Duke was a man of that magnanimity and prudence, understood so well which way men were to be wheedled, or destroyed, and such were the foundations that he had laid in a short time, that had he not had those two great armies upon his back, and a fierce distemper upon his body, he had overcome all difficulties and brought his designs to perfection. That the foundations which he had laid were plausible appeared by the patience of his subjects in Romagna, who held out for him a complete month, though they knew he was at death's door, and unlikely ever to come out of Rome, to which place, though the Baglioni, the Vitelli, and the Ursini returned, seeing there was no likelihood of his recovery, yet they could not gain any of his party, nor debauch them to their side. It is possible he was not able to put who he pleased into the Pontifical chair, yet he had power enough to keep any man out who he thought was his enemy; but had it been his fortune to have been well when his father Alexander died, all things had succeeded to his mind. He told me himself, about the time that Julius XI was created, that he had considered well the accidents that might befall him upon the death of his father, and provided against them all, only he did not imagine that at his death he should be so near it himself. Upon serious examination, therefore, of the whole conduct of Duke Valentine, I see nothing to be reprehended; it seems rather proper to me to propose him, as I have done, as an example for the imitation of all such as by the favour of fortune, or the supplies of other princes, have got into the saddle; for his mind being so large, and his intentions so high, he could not do otherwise, and nothing could have opposed the greatness and wisdom of his designs but his own infirmity and the death of his father. He, therefore, who thinks it necessary in the minority of his dominion to secure himself against his enemies, to gain himself friends; to overcome, whether by force or by fraud; to make himself beloved or feared by his people; to be followed and reverenced by his soldiers; to destroy and exterminate such as would do him injury; to repeal and suppress old laws, and introduce new; to be severe, grateful, magnanimous, liberal, cashier and disband such of his army as were unfaithful, and put new in their places; manage himself so in his alliances with kings and princes that all of them should be either obliged to requite him or afraid to offend him: he, I say, cannot find a fresher or better model than the actions of this prince. If in anything he is to be condemned, it is in suffering the election of Julius XI, which was much to his prejudice; for though, as is said before, he might be unable to make the Pope as he pleased, yet it was in his power to have put any one by, and he ought never to have consented to the election of any of the cardinals whom he had formerly offended, or who, after their promotion, were like to be jealous of him; for men are as mischievous for fear as for hated. Those cardinals which he had disobliged were, among others, the cardinals of St. Peter ad Vincula, Collonno St. George, and Ascanius. The rest, if any of them were advanced to the Papacy, might well be afraid of him, except the Spanish

cardinals and the cardinal of Roan; the Spaniards by
reason of their obligations and alliance, and the other
by reason of his interest in the kingdom of France.
Wherefore, above all things, the Duke should have made
a Spanish cardinal Pope; and if that could not have been
done, he should rather have consented to the election
of Roan than St. Peter ad Vincula; for it is weakness to
believe that among great persons new obligations can
obliterate old injuries and disgusts. So that in the election of this Julius XI Duke Valentine committed an error
that was the cause of his utter destruction.

CHAPTER 8

Of such as have arrived at their Dominion
by wicked and unjustifiable means

Now because there are two ways from a private person to
become a prince, which ways are not altogether to be
attributed either to fortune or management, I think it not
convenient to pretermit them, though of one of them I
may speak more largely where occasion is offered to treat
more particularly of Republics. One of the ways is, when
one is advanced to the sovereignty by any illegal nefarious
means; the other, when a citizen by the favour and
partiality of his fellow-citizens is made prince of his
country. I shall speak of the first in this chapter, and justify
what I say by two examples, one ancient, the other
modern, without entering further into the merits of the
cause, as judging them sufficient for any man who is
necessitated to follow them. Agathocles, the Sicilian, not
only from a private, but from a vile and abject, condition
was made king of Syracuse; and being but the son of a
potter, he continued the dissoluteness of his life through
all the degrees of his fortune; nevertheless, his vices were
accompanied with such courage and activity that he
applied himself to the wars, by which, and his great
industry, he came at length to the pretor of Syracuse.
Being settled in that dignity, and having concluded to

make himself prince, and hold that by violence, without obligation to anybody, which was conferred upon him by consent, he settled an intelligence with Amilcar the Carthaginian, who was then at the head of an army in Sicily, and calling the people and Senate of Syracuse together one morning, as if he had been to consult them in some matter of importance to the State, upon a signal appointed he caused all his soldiers to kill all the senators and the most wealthy of the people; after whose death he usurped and possessed the dominion of that city without any obstruction; and though afterwards he lost two great battles to the Carthaginians, and at length was besieged, yet he was not only able to defend that city, but leaving part of his forces for the security of that, with the rest he transported into Africa, and ordered things so that in a short time he relieved Syracuse, and reduced the Carthaginians into such extreme necessity that they were glad to make peace with him, and contenting themselves with Africa, leave Sicily to Agathocles. He then who examines the exploits and conduct of Agathocles will find little or nothing that may be attributed to fortune, seeing he rose not, as is said before, by the favour of any man, but by the steps and gradations of war, with a thousand difficulties and dangers having gotten that government, which he maintained afterwards with as many noble achievements. Nevertheless it cannot be called virtue in him to kill his fellow-citizens, betray his friends, to be without faith, without pity, or religion; these are ways may get a man empire, but no glory or reputation. Yet if the wisdom of Agathocles be considered, his dexterity in encountering and overcoming of dangers, his courage in supporting and surmounting his misfortunes, I do not see why he should be held inferior to the best captains of his time. But his unbounded cruelty and barbarous inhumanity, added to a million of other vices, will not permit that he be numbered amongst the most excellent men. So then, that which he performed cannot justly be attributed to either fortune or virtue; for he did all himself, without either the one or the other. In our days, under the Papacy of Alexander VI, Oliverotto da Fermo being left young many years since by his parents, was brought up by his uncle by the mother's side, called John Fogliani, and in his youth listed a soldier under Paulo Vitelli, that having improved himself by his discipline, he might be capable of some eminent command. Paulo being dead, he served under Vitellezzo, his brother, and in a short time by the acuteness of his parts and the briskness of his courage, became one of the best officers in his army. But thinking it beneath him to continue in any man's service, he conspired with some of his fellow-citizens of Fermo (to whom the servitude of their country was more agreeable than its liberty) by the help of Vitellesco to seize upon Fermo. In order to which, he wrote a letter to his uncle John Fogliano, importing that, having been absent many years, he had thoughts of visiting him and Fermo, and taking some little diversion in the place where he was born, and because the design of his service had been only the gaining of honour, that his fellow-citizens might see his time had not been ill-spent, he desired admission for a hundred horse of his friends and his equipage, and begged of him that he would take care they might be honourably received, which would redound not only to his honour, but his uncle's, who had had the bringing him up. John was not wanting in any office to his nephew, and having caused him to be nobly received, he lodged him in his own house, where he continued some days, preparing in the meantime what was necessary to the execution of his wicked design. He made a great entertainment, to which he invited John Fogliani and all the chief citizens in the town. About the end of the treatment when they were entertaining one another, as is usual at such times, Oliverotto very subtilly promoted certain grave discourses about the greatness of Pope Alexander and Cæsar his son, and of their designs. John and the rest replying freely to what was said, Oliverotto smiled, and told them those were points to be argued more privately, and thereupon removing into a chamber, his uncle and the rest of his fellow-citizens followed. They were scarce sat down before soldiers (which were concealed about the room) came forth and killed all of them, and the uncle among the rest. After the murder was committed, Oliverotto mounted on horseback, rode about, and rummaged the whole town, having besieged the chief magistrate in his palace; so that for fear all people submitted, and he established a government of which he made himself head. Having put such to death as were discontented, and in any capacity of doing him hurt, he fortified himself with new laws, both military and civil, insomuch as in a year's time he had not only fixed himself in Fermo, but was become terrible to all that were about him; and he would have been as hard as Agathocles to be supplanted, had he not suffered himself to have been circumvented by Cæsar Borgia, when at Singalia (as aforesaid) he took the Ursini and Vitelli; where also he himself was taken a year after his parricide was committed, and strangled with his master Vitellozzo, from whom he had learned all his good qualities and evil.

It may seem wonderful to some people how it should come to pass that Agathocles, and such as he, after so many treacheries and acts of inhumanity, should live quietly in their own country so long, defend themselves so well against foreign enemies, and none of their subjects conspire against them at home, seeing several others, by reason of their cruelty, have not been able, even in times of peace as well as war, to defend their government. I conceive it fell out according as their cruelty was well or ill applied; I say well applied (if that word may be added to an ill action), and it may be called so when committed but once, and that of necessity for one's own preservation, but never repeated afterwards, and even then converted as much as possible to the benefit of the subjects. Ill applied are such cruelties as are but few in the beginning, but in time do rather multiply than decrease. Those who are guilty of the first do receive assistance sometimes both from God and man, and Agathocles is an instance. But the others cannot possibly subsist long. From whence it is to be observed, that he who usurps the government of any State is to execute and put in practice all the cruelties which he thinks material at once, that he may have no occasion to renew them often, but that by his discontinuance he may mollify the people, and by his benefits bring them over to his side. He who does otherwise, whether for fear or ill counsel, is obliged to be always ready with his knife in his hand; for he can never repose any confidence in his subjects, whilst they, by reason of his fresh and continued inhumanities, cannot be secure against him. So then injuries are to be committed all at once, that the last being the less, the distaste may be likewise the less; but benefits should be distilled by drops, that the relish may be the greater. Above all, a prince is so to behave himself towards his subjects that neither good fortune nor bad should be able to alter him; for being once assaulted with adversity, you have no time to do mischief; and the good which you do, does you no good, being looked upon as forced, and so no thanks to be due for it.

CHAPTER 9

Of Civil Principality

I shall speak now of the other way, when a principal citizen, not by wicked contrivance or intolerable violence, is made sovereign of his country, which may be called a civil principality, and is not to be attained by either virtue or fortune alone, but by a lucky sort of craft; this man, I say, arrives at the government by the favour of the people or nobility, for in all cities the meaner and the better sort of citizens are of different humours, and it proceeds from hence that the common people are not willing to be commanded and oppressed by the great ones, and the great ones are not to be satisfied without it. From this diversity of appetite one of these three effects do arise—principality, liberty, or licentiousness. Principality is caused either by the people or the great ones, as either the one or the other has occasion; the great ones, finding themselves unable to resist the popular torrent, do many times unanimously confer their whole authority upon one person, and create him prince, that under his protection they may be quiet and secure. The people, on the other side, when overpowered by their adversaries, do the same thing, transmitting their power to a single person, who is made king for their better defence. He who arrives at the sovereignty by the

assistance of the great ones preserves it with more difficulty than he who is advanced by the people, because
he has about him many of his old associates, who,
thinking themselves his equals, are not to be directed
and managed as he would have them. But he that is
preferred by the people stands alone without equals, and
has nobody, or very few, about him but what are ready
to obey; moreover, the grandees are hardly to be satisfied
without injury to others, which is otherwise with the
people, because their designs are more reasonable than
the designs of the great ones, which are fixed upon
commanding and oppressing altogether, whilst the
people endeavour only to defend and secure themselves.
Moreover, where the people are adverse the prince can
never be safe, by reason of their numbers; whereas the
great ones are but few, and by consequence not so
dangerous. The worst that a prince can expect from an
injured and incensed people is to be deserted; but, if the
great ones be provoked, he is not only to fear abandoning,
but conspiracy and banding against him; for the greater
sort being more provident and cunning, they look out in
time to their own safety, and make their interest with
the person who they hope will overcome. Besides, the
prince is obliged to live always with one and the same
people; but with the grandees he is under no such obligation, for he may create and degrade, advance and
remove them as he pleases. But for the better explication
of this part, I say, that these great men are to be considered two ways especially; that is, whether in the manner
of their administration they do wholly follow the fortune
and interest of the prince, or whether they do otherwise.
Those who devote themselves entirely to his business,
and are not rapacious, are to be valued and preferred.
Those who are more remiss, and will not stick to their
prince, do it commonly upon two motives, either out of

laziness or fear (and in those cases they may be employed, especially if they be wise and of good counsel, because, if affairs prosper, thou gainest honour thereby; if they miscarry, thou needest not to fear them) or upon ambition and design, and that is a token that their thoughts are more intent upon their own advantage than thine. Of these a prince ought always to have a more than ordinary care, and order them as if they were enemies professed; for in his distress they will be sure to set him forwards, and do what they can to destroy him. He, therefore, who comes to be prince by the favour and suffrage of the people is obliged to keep them his friends, which (their desire being nothing but freedom from oppression) may be easily done. But he that is preferred by the interest of the nobles against the minds of the commons, is, above all things, to endeavour to ingratiate with the people, which will be as the other if he undertakes their protection; and men receiving good offices, where they expected ill, are endeared by the surprise, and become better affected to their benefactor than perhaps they would have been had he been made prince by their immediate favour. There are many ways of insinuating with the people of which no certain rule can be given, because they vary according to the diversity of the subject, and therefore I shall pass them at this time, concluding with this assertion—that it is necessary, above all things, that a prince preserves the affections of his people, otherwise, in any exigence, he has no refuge or remedy. Nabides, Prince of the Spartans, sustained all Greece and a victorious army of the Romans, and defended the government and country against them all; and to do that great action it was sufficient for him to secure himself against the machinations of a few; whereas, if the people had been his enemy, that would not have done it. Let no man impugn my opinion with that old saying, "He that builds upon the people builds upon the sand." That is true, indeed, when a citizen of private condition relies upon the people, and persuades himself that when the magistrate or his adversary goes about to oppress him they will bring him off, in which case many precedents may be produced, and particularly the Gracchi in Rome, and Georgio Scali in Florence. But if the prince that builds upon them knows how to command, and be a man of courage, not dejected in adversity, nor deficient in his other preparations, but keeps up the spirits of his people by his own valour and conduct, he shall never be deserted by them, nor find his foundations laid in a wrong place.

These kind of governments are most tottering and uncertain when the prince strains of a sudden, and passes, as at one leap, from a civil to an absolute power; and the reason is, because they either command and act by themselves or by the ministry and mediation of the magistrate. In this last case their authority is weaker and more ticklish, because it depends much upon the pleasure and concurrence of the chief officers, who, in time of adversity especially, can remove them easily, either by neglecting or resisting their commands; nor is there any way for such a prince, in the perplexity of his affairs, to establish a tyranny, because those citizens and subjects who used to exercise the magistracy retain still such power and influence upon the people, that they will not infringe the laws to obey his; and in time of danger he shall always want such as he can trust. So that a prince is not to take his measures according to what he sees in times of peace, when of the subjects, having nothing to do but to be governed, every one runs, every one promises, and every one dies for him when death is at a distance; but when times are tempestuous, and the ship of the State has need of the help and assistance of the subject, there are but few will expose themselves, and this experiment is the more dangerous because it can be practised but once. So, then, a prince who is provident and wise ought to carry himself so that in all places, times, and occasions the people may have need of his administration and regiment, and ever after they shall be faithful and true.

CHAPTER 10

How the strength of all Principalities is to
be computed

To any man that examines the nature of principalities, it
is worthy his consideration whether a prince has power
and territory enough to subsist by himself, or whether he
needs the assistance and protection of other people. To
clear the point a little better, I think those princes capable
of ruling who are able, either by the numbers of their men
or the greatness of their wealth, to raise a complete army,
and bid battle to any that shall invade them; and those I
think depend upon others, who of themselves dare not
meet their enemy in the field, but are forced to keep within
their bounds and defend them as well they can. Of the
first we have spoken already, and shall say more as occasion
is presented. Of the second no more can be said, but to
advise such princes to strengthen and fortify the capital
town in their dominions, and not to trouble themselves
with the whole country; and whoever shall do that, and
in other things manage himself with the subjects as I have
described, and perhaps shall do hereafter, shall with great
caution be invaded; for men are generally wary and tender
of enterprising anything that is difficult, and no great easi-
ness is to be found in attacking a town well fortified and
provided, where the prince is not hated by the people.

The towns in Germany are many of them free; though their country and district be but small, yet they obey the Emperor but when they please, and are in no awe either of him or any other prince of the empire, because they are all so well fortified. Every one looks upon the taking of any one of them as a work of great difficulty and time, their walls being so strong, their ditches so deep, their works so regular and well provided with cannon, and their stores and magazines always furnished for a twelve-month. Besides which, for the aliment and sustenance of the people, and that they may be no burden to the public, they have workhouses where, for a year together, the poor may be employed in such things as are the nerves and life of that city, and sustain themselves by their labour. Military discipline and exercises are likewise in much request there, and many laws and good customs they have to maintain them.

A prince then who has a city well fortified, and the affections of his people, is not easily to be molested, and he that does molest him is like to repent it; for the affairs of this world are so various, it is almost impossible for any army to lie quietly a whole year before a town without interruption. If any objects that the people having houses and possessions out of the town will not have patience to see them plundered and burned, and that charity to themselves will make them forget their prince, I answer, that a wise and dexterous prince will easily evade those difficulties by encouraging his subjects and persuading them, sometimes their troubles will not be long; sometimes inculcating and possessing them with the cruelty of the enemy; and sometimes by correcting and securing himself nimbly of such as appear too turbulent and audacious. Moreover, the usual practice is for the enemy to plunder and set the country on fire at their first coming, whilst every man's spirit is high and fixed upon defence;

so that the prince needs not concern himself, nor be fearful of that, for those mischiefs are passed, and inconveniencies received, and when the people in three or four days' time begin to be cool, and consider things soberly, they will find there is no remedy, and join more cordially with the prince, looking upon him as under an obligation to them for having sacrificed their houses and estates in his defence. And the nature of man is such to take as much pleasure in having obliged another as in being obliged himself. Wherefore, all things fairly considered, it is no such hard matter for a prince not only to gain, but to retain, the affection of his subjects, and make them patient of a long siege, if he be wise and provident, and takes care they want nothing either for their livelihood or defence.

CHAPTER 11

Of Ecclesiastical Principalities

There remains nothing of this nature to be discoursed but of Ecclesiastical Principalities, about which the greatest difficulty is to get into possession, because they are gained either by fortune or virtue, but kept without either, being supported by ancient statutes universally received in the Christian Church, which are of such power and authority they do keep their prince in his dignity, let his conversation or conduct be what it will. These are the only persons who have lands and do not defend them; subjects, and do not govern them; and yet their lands are not taken from them, though they never defend them; nor their subjects dissatisfied, though they never regard them: so that these principalities are the happiest and most secure in the world, by being managed by a supernatural power, above the wisdom and contrivance of man. I shall speak no more of them, for, being set up and continued by God Himself, it would be great presumption in any man who should undertake to dispute them. Nevertheless, if it should be questioned how it came to pass that in temporal things the Church is arrived at that height, seeing that, before Alexander's time, the Italian princes, not only such as were sovereigns, but every baron and lord, how inconsiderable soever in temporal affairs, esteemed of them but little; yet, since it has been able not only to startle and confront the King of France, but to drive him out of Italy, and to ruin the Venetians, the reason of which, though already well known, I think it not superfluous to revive in some measure.

Before Charles, King of France, passed himself into Italy, that province was under the empire of the Pope, the Venetians, the King of Naples, Duke of Milan, and the Florentines. It was the interest of these potentates to have a care, some of them that no foreign prince should come with an army into Italy, and some that none among themselves should usurp upon the other. Those of whom the rest were concerned to be most jealous were the Pope and the Venetians; to restrain the Venetians all the rest were used to confederate, as in the defence of Ferrara. To keep under the Pope, the Roman barons contributed much, who, being divided into two factions (the Ursini and Colonnesi, in perpetual contention, with their arms constantly in their hands under the very nose of the Pope), they kept the pontifical power very low and infirm; and although now and then there happened a courageous Pope, as Sextus, yet neither his courage, wisdom, nor fortune was able to disentangle him from those incommodities, and the shortness of their reign was the reason thereof; for ten years' time, which was as much as any of them reigned, was scarce sufficient for the suppression of either of the parties; and when the Colonnesi, as a man may say, were almost extinct, a new enemy sprang up against the Ursini, which revived the Colonnesi and re-established them again. This emulation and animosity at home was the cause the Pope was no more formidable in Italy. After this, Alexander VI was advanced to the Papacy, who, more than all that had ever been before him, demonstrated what a

Pope with money and power was able to do. Having taken advantage of the French invasion, by the ministry and conduct of Duke Valentine, he performed all that I have mentioned elsewhere among the actions of the said Duke. And though his design was not so much to advantage the Church as to aggrandize the Duke, yet what he did for the one turned afterwards to the benefit of the other; for, the Pope being dead and Valentine extinct, what both of them had got devolved upon the Church. After him Julius succeeded, and found the Church in a flourishing condition. Romagna was wholly in its possession, the barons of Rome exterminated and gone, and their factions suppressed by Pope Alexander, and, besides, a way opened for raising and hoarding of money never practised before; which way Julius improving rather than otherwise, he began to entertain thoughts, not only of conquering Bologna, but mastering the Venetians and forcing the French out of Italy; all which great enterprises succeeding, it added much to his honour that he impropriated nothing, but gave all to the Church. He maintained also the Colonnesi and Ursini in the same condition as he found them; and though in case of sedition there were those ready on both sides to have headed them, yet there were two considerations which kept them at peace: one was the greatness of the Church, which kept them in awe; the other was their want of cardinals, which indeed was the original of their discontent, and will never cease till some of them be advanced to that dignity; for by them the parties in Rome and without are maintained, and the barons obliged to defend them. So that the ambition of the prelates is the cause of all the dissension and tumults among the barons.

His present Holiness Pope Leo had the happiness to be elected at a time when it was most powerful, and it is hoped, if they made the Church great by their arms, he, by the integrity of his conversation and a thousand other virtues, will enlarge it much more, and make it more venerable and august.

CHAPTER 12

How many Forms there are of Military
Discipline, and of those Soldiers which are
called Mercenary

Having spoken particularly of the several sorts of principalities, as I proposed in the beginning; considered in
part the reasons of their constitution and their evil, and
the ways which many have taken to acquire and preserve
them; it remains that I proceed now in a general way
upon such things as may conduce to the offence or
defence of either of them.

We have declared before that it is not only expedient
but necessary for a prince to take care his foundations
be good, otherwise his fabric will be sure to fail.

The principal foundations of all States—new, old, or
mixed—are good laws and good arms; and because there
cannot be good laws where there are not good arms, and
where the arms are good there must be good laws, I shall
pass by the laws and discourse of the arms.

I say the arms, then, with which a prince defends
his State are his own, mercenary, auxiliary, or mixed.
The mercenary and auxiliary are unprofitable and
dangerous, and that prince who founds the duration of
his government upon his mercenary forces shall never

be firm or secure; for they are divided, ambitious, un-disciplined, unfaithful, insolent to their friends, abject to their enemies, without fear of God or faith to men; so the ruin of that person who trusts to them is no longer protracted than the attempt is deferred; in time of peace they divorce you, in time of war they desert you, and the reason is because it is not love nor any principle of honour that keeps them in the field; it is only their pay, and that is not a consideration strong enough to prevail with them to die for you; whilst you have no service to employ them in, they are excellent soldiers; but tell them of an engagement, and they will either disband before or run away in the battle.

And to evince this would require no great pains; seeing the ruin of Italy proceeded from no other cause than that for several years together it had reposed itself upon mercenary arms, which forces it is possible may have formerly done service to some particular person, and behaved themselves well enough among one another; but no sooner were they attacked by a powerful foreigner, but they discovered themselves, and showed what they were to the world. Hence it was that Charles VII chalked out his own way into. Italy; and that person was in the right who affirmed our own faults were the cause of our miseries. But it was not those faults he believed, but those I have mentioned, which being committed most eminently by princes, they suffered most remarkably in the punishment. But to come closer to the point, and give you a clearer prospect of the imperfection and infelicity of those forces. The great officers of these mercenaries are men of great courage, or otherwise; if the first, you can never be safe, for they always aspire to make themselves great, either by supplanting of you who is their master, or oppressing of other people whom you desired to have preserved; and, on the other side, if the commanders be not courageous, you are ruined again. If it should be urged that all generals will do the same, whether mercenaries or others, I would answer, that all war is managed either by a prince or republic. The prince is obliged to go in person, and perform the office of general himself; the republic must depute some one of her choice citizens, who is to be changed if he carries himself ill; if he behaves himself well he is to be continued, but so straitened and circumscribed by his commission that he may not transgress. And indeed experience tells us that princes alone, and commonwealths alone, with their own private forces have performed great things, whereas mercenaries do nothing but hurt. Besides, a martial commonwealth that stands upon its own legs and maintains itself by its own prowess is not easily usurped, and falls not so readily under the obedience of one of their fellow-citizens as where all the forces are foreign. Rome and Sparta maintained their own liberty for many years together by their own forces and arms. The Swiss are more martial than their neighbours, and by consequence more free. Of the danger of mercenary forces we have an ancient example in the Carthaginians, who, after the end of their first war with the Romans, had like to have been ruined and overrun by their own mercenaries, though their own citizens commanded them.

After the death of Epaminondas the Thebans made Philip of Macedon their general, who defeated their enemies and enslaved themselves. Upon the death of Duke Philip the Milanese entertained Francesco Sforza against the Venetians, and Francesco, having worsted the enemy at Caravaggio, joined himself with him, with design to have mastered his masters. Francesco's father was formerly in the service of Joan, Queen of Naples, and on a sudden marched away from her with his army and left her utterly destitute, so that she was constrained to throw herself under the protection of the King of Arragon; and though the Venetians and Florentines both have lately enlarged their dominion by employing these forces, and their generals have rather advanced than enslaved them, I answer that the Florentines may impute it to their good fortune, because of such of their generals as they might have rationally feared some had no victories to encourage them, others were obstructed, and others turned their ambition another way. He that was not victorious was Giovanni Acuto, whose fidelity could not be known because he had no opportunity to break it, but everybody knows, had he succeeded, the Florentines had been all at his mercy. Sforza had always the Braccheschi in opposition, and they were reciprocally an impediment the one to the other. Francesco turned his ambition upon Lombardy, Braccio upon the Church and the kingdom of Naples. But to speak of more modern occurrences. The Florentines made Paul Vitelli their general, a wise man, and one who from a private fortune had raised himself to a great reputation, Had Paul taken Pisa, nobody can be insensible how the Florentines must have comported with him; for should he have quitted their service and taken pay of their enemy they had been lost without remedy, and to have continued him in that power had been in time to have made him their master. If the progress of the Venetians be considered, they will be found to have acted securely and honourably whilst their affairs were managed by their own forces (which was before they attempted anything upon the *terra firma*); then all was done by the gentlemen and common people of that city, and they did very great things; but when they began to enterprise at land, they began to abate of their old reputation and discipline and to degenerate into the customs of Italy; and when they began to

conquer first upon the continent, having no great territory, and their reputation being formidable abroad, there
was no occasion that they should be much afraid of their
officers; but afterwards, when they began to extend their
empire under the command of Carmignola, then it was
they became sensible of their error; for having found
him to be a great captain by their victories, under his
conduct, against the Duke of Milan, perceiving him afterwards grow cool and remiss in their service, they
concluded no more great things were to be expected
from him; and being neither willing, nor indeed able, to
take away his commission, for fear of losing what they
had got, they were constrained for their own security to
put him to death. Their generals after him were
Bartolomeo da Bergamo, Roberto da San Severino, and
the Conte de Pitigliano, and such as they, under whose
conduct the Venetians were more like to lose than to
gain, as it happened not long after at Vaila, where in one
battle they lost as much as they had been gaining eight
hundred years with incredible labour and difficulty;
which is not strange, if it be considered that by those
kind of forces the conquests are slow, and tedious, and
weak; but their losses are rapid and wonderful. And
because I am come with my examples into Italy, where
for many years all things have been managed by
mercenary armies, I shall lay my discourse a little higher,
that their original and progress being rendered more
plain, they may with more ease be regulated and
corrected. You must understand that in later times, when
the Roman empire began to decline in Italy, and the
Pope to take upon him authority in temporal affairs, Italy
became divided into several States; for many of the great
cities took arms against their nobility, who, having been
formerly favoured by the emperors, kept the people
under oppression, against which the Church opposed, to

gain to itself a reputation and interest in temporal affairs; other cities were subdued by their citizens, who made themselves princes; so that Italy, upon the translation of the empire, being fallen into the hands of the Pope and some other commonwealths, and those priests and citizens unacquainted with the use and exercise of arms, they began to take foreigners into their pay. The first man who gave reputation to these kind of forces was Alberigo da Como of Romagna; among the rest, Braccio and Sforza (the two great arbiters of Italy in their time) were brought up under his discipline, after whom succeeded the rest who commanded the armies in Italy to our days; and the end of their great discipline and conduct was, that Italy was overrun by Charles, pillaged by Louis violated by Ferrand, and defamed by the Swiss. The order which they observed was, first to take away the reputation from the foot and appropriate it to themselves; and this they did, because their dominion being but small, and to be maintained by their own industry, a few foot could not do their business, and a great body they could not maintain. Hereupon they changed their militia into horse, which, being digested into troops, they sustained and rewarded themselves with the commands, and by degrees this way of cavalry was grown so much in fashion that in an army of 20,000 men there were scarce 2,000 foot to be found. Besides, they endeavoured with all possible industry to prevent trouble or fear, either to themselves or their soldiers, and their way was by killing nobody in fight, only taking one another prisoners, and dismissing them afterwards without either prejudice or ransom. When they were in leaguer before a town, they shot not rudely amongst them in the night, nor did they in the town disturb them with any sallies in their camp; no approaches or intrenchments were made at unseasonable hours, and nothing of lying in the field when winter came on; and all these things did not happen by any negligence in their officers, but were part of their discipline, and introduced, as is said before, to ease the poor soldier both of labour and danger, by which practices they have brought Italy both into slavery and contempt.

CHAPTER 13

Of Auxiliaries, Mixed, and Natural Soldiers

Auxiliaries (which are another sort of unprofitable soldiers) are when some potent prince is called in to your assistance and defence; as was done not long since by Pope Julius, who, in his enterprise of Ferrara, having seen the sad experience of his mercenary army, betook himself to auxiliaries, and capitulated with Ferrand, King of Spain, that he should come with his forces to his relief. These armies may do well enough for themselves, but he who invites them is sure to be a sufferer; for if they be beaten, he is sure to be a loser; if they succeed, he is left at their discretion; and though ancient histories are full of examples of this kind, yet I shall keep to that of Pope Julius XI, as one still fresh in our memory, whose expedition against Ferrara was very rash and inconsiderate, in that he put all into the hands of a stranger; but his good fortune presented him with a third accident, which prevented his reaping the fruit of his imprudent election; for his subsidiary troops being broke at Ravenna, and the Swiss coming in and beating off the victors, beyond all expectation he escaped being a prisoner to his enemies, because they also were defeated, and to his auxiliary friends, because he had conquered by other people's arms. The Florentines, being destitute of soldiers, hired 10,000 French for the reduction of Pisa, by which counsel they ran themselves into greater danger than ever they had done in all their troubles before. The Emperor of Constantinople, in opposition to his neighbours, sent 10,000 Turks into Greece, which could not be got out again when the war was at an end, but gave the first beginning to the servitude and captivity which those infidels brought upon that country. He, then, who has no mind to overcome may make use of these forces, for they are much more dangerous than the mercenary, and will ruin you out of hand, because they are always unanimous, and at the command of other people; whereas the mercenaries, after they have gotten a victory, must have longer time and more occasion before they can do you a mischief, in respect they are not one body, but made up out of several countries entertained into your pay, to which, if you add a general of your own, they cannot suddenly assume so much authority as will be able lo do you any prejudice. In short, it is cowardice and sloth that is to be feared in the mercenaries, and courage and activity in the auxiliaries. A wise prince, therefore, never made use of these forces, but committed himself to his own, choosing rather to be overcome with them than to conquer with the other, because he cannot think that a victory which is obtained by other people's arms. I shall make no scruple to produce Cæsar Borgia for an example. This Duke invaded Romagna with an army of auxiliaries, consisting wholly of French, by whose assistance he took Imola and Furli; but finding them afterwards to totter in their faith, and himself insecure, he betook himself to mercenaries as the less dangerous of the two, and entertained the Ursini and Vitelli into his pay; finding them also irresolute, unfaithful, and dangerous, he dismissed them, and for the future employed none but his own. From hence we may collect the difference betwixt these two sorts of forces, if we consider the difference in the Duke's reputation when the Ursini and Vitelli were in his service and when he had no soldiers but his own. When he began to stand upon his own legs his renown began to increase, and, indeed, before his esteem was not so great till everybody found him absolute master of his own army.

Having begun my examples in Italy I am unwilling to leave it, especially whilst it supplies us with such as are fresh in our memory; yet I cannot pass by Micro of Syracuse, whom I have mentioned before. This person, being made general of the Syracusan army, quickly discovered the mercenary militia was not to be relied upon, their officers being qualified like ours in Italy, and, finding that he could neither continue nor discharge them securely, he ordered things so that they were ail cut to pieces, and then prosecuted the war with his own forces alone, without any foreign assistance. To this purpose the Old Testament affords us a figure not altogether improper. When David presented himself to Saul, and offered his service against Goliah, the champion of the Philistines, Saul, to encourage him, accoutred him in his own arms; but David, having tried them on, excused himself, pretending they were unfit, and that with them he should not be able to manage himself; wherefore he desired he might go forth against the enemy with his own arms only, which were his sling and his sword. The sum of all is, the arms of other people are commonly unfit, and either too wide, or too strait, or too cumbersome.

Charles VII, the father of Louis XI, having by his fortune and courage redeemed his country out of the hands of the English, began to understand the necessity of having soldiers of his own, and erected a militia at home, to consist of horse as well as foot, after which his son, King Louis, cashiered his own foot and took the Swiss into his pay, which error being followed by his successors (as is visible to this day) is the occasion of all the dangers to which that kingdom of France is still obnoxious; for, having advanced the reputation of the Swiss, he villified his own people by disbanding the foot entirely, and accustoming his horse so much to engage with other soldiers that, fighting still in conjunction with the Swiss, they began to believe they could do nothing without them; hence it proceeds that the French are not able to do anything against the Swiss, and without them they will venture upon nothing; so that the French army is mixed, consists of mercenaries and natives, and is much better than either mercenaries or auxiliaries alone, but much worse than if it were entirely natural, as this example testifies abundantly; for doubtless France would be insuperable if Charles's establishment was made use of and improved. But the imprudence of man begins many things which, savouring of present good, conceal the poison that is latent, as I said before of the hectic fever; wherefore, if he who is raised to any sovereignty foresees not a mischief till it falls upon his head, he is not to be reckoned a wise prince, and truly that is a particular blessing of God bestowed upon few people. If we reflect upon the first cause of the ruin of the Roman empire, it will be found to begin at their entertaining the Goths into their service, for thereby they weakened and enervated their own native courage, and, as it were, transfused it into them.

I conclude, therefore, that without having proper and peculiar forces of his own, no prince is secure, but depends wholly upon fortune, as having no natural and intrinsic strength to sustain him in adversity; and it was always the opinion and position of wise men, that nothing is so infirm and unstable as the name of power not founded upon forces of its own. Those forces are composed of your subjects, your citizens, or servants; all the rest are either mercenaries or auxiliaries: and as to the manner of ordering and disciplining these domestics, it will not be hard if the orders which I have prescribed be perused, and the way considered which Philip the father of Alexander the Great, and many other princes and republics, have used in the like cases, to which orders and establishments I do wholly refer you.

CHAPTER 14

The Duty of a Prince in relation to his Militia

A Prince, then, is to have no other design, nor thought, nor study but war and the arts and disciplines of it; for, indeed, that is the only profession worthy of a prince, and is of so much importance that it not only preserves those who are born princes in their patrimonies, but advances men of private condition to that honourable degree. On the other side, it is frequently seen, when princes have addicted themselves more to delicacy and softness than to arms, they have lost all, and been driven out of their States; for the principal thing which deprives or gains a man authority is the neglect or profession of that art. Francesco Sforza, by his experience in war, of a private person made himself Duke of Milan, and his children, seeking to avoid the fatigues and incommodities thereof, of dukes became private men; for, among other evils and inconveniences which attend when you are ignorant in war, it makes you contemptible, which is a scandal a prince ought with all diligence to avoid, for reasons I shall name hereafter; besides, betwixt a potent and an impotent, a vigilant and a negligent prince, there is no proportion, it being unreasonable that a martial and generous person should be subject willingly to one that is weak and remiss, or that those who are careless and effeminate should be safe amongst those who are military and active; for the one is too insolent and the other too captious ever to do anything well together: so that a prince unacquainted with the discipline of war, besides other infelicities to which he is exposed, cannot be beloved by, nor confident in, his armies. He never, therefore, ought to relax his thoughts from the exercises of war not so much as in time of peace; and, indeed, then he should employ his thoughts more studiously therein than in war itself, which may be done two ways, by the application of the body and the mind, As to his bodily application, or matter of action, besides that he is obliged to keep his armies in good discipline and exercise, he ought to inure himself to sports, and by hunting and hawking, and such like recreation, accustom his body to hardship, and hunger, and thirst, and at the same time inform himself of the coasts and situation of the country, the bigness and elevation of the mountains, the largeness and avenues of the valleys, the extent of the plains, the nature of the rivers and fens, which is to be done with great curiosity; and this knowledge is useful two ways, for hereby he not only learns to know his own country and to provide better for its defence, but it prepares and adapts him, by observing their situations, to comprehend the situations of other countries, which will perhaps be necessary for him to discover; for the hills, the vales, the plains, the rivers, and the marshes (for example, in Tuscany), have a certain similitude and resemblance with those in other provinces; so that, by the knowledge of one, we may easily imagine the rest; and that prince who is defective in this, wants the most necessary qualification of a general; for by knowing the country, he knows how to beat up his enemy, take up his quarters, march his armies, draw up his men, and besiege a town with advantage. In the character which historians give of Philopomenes, Prince of Achaia, one of his great commendations is, that in time of peace he thought of nothing but military affairs, and when he was in company with his friends in the country, he would many times stop suddenly and expostulate with them: If the enemy were upon that hill, and our army where we are, which would have the advantage of the ground? How could we come at them with most security? If we would draw off, how might we do it best? Or, if they would retreat, how might we follow? So that as he was travelling, he would propose all the accidents to which an army was subject; he would hear their opinion, give them his own, and reinforce it with arguments; and this he did so frequently, that by continual practice and a constant intention of his thoughts upon that business, he brought himself to that perfection, no accident could happen, no inconvenience could occur to an army, but he could presently redress it. But as to the exercise of the mind, a prince is to do that by diligence in history and solemn consideration of the actions of the most excellent men, by observing how they demeaned themselves in the wars, examining the grounds and reasons of their victories and losses, that he may be able to avoid the one and imitate the other; and above all, to keep close to the example of some great captain of old (if any such occurs in his reading), and not only to make him his pattern, but to have all his actions perpetually in his mind, as it was said Alexander did by Achilles, Cæsar by Alexander, Scipio by Cyrus. And whoever reads the life of Cyrus, written by Xenophon, will find how much Scipio advantaged his renown by that imitation, and how much in modesty, affability, humanity, and liberality he framed himself to the description which Xenophon had given him. A wise prince, therefore, is to observe all these rules, and never be idle in time of peace, but employ himself therein with all his industry, that in his adversity he may reap the fruit of it, and when fortune frowns, be ready to defy her.

CHAPTER 15

Of such things as render Men (especially Princes) worthy of Blame or Applause

It remains now that we see in what manner a prince ought to comport with his subjects and friends; and because many have written of this subject before, it may perhaps seem arrogant in me, especially considering that in my discourse I shall deviate from the opinion of other men. But my intention being to write for the benefit and advantage of him who understands, I thought it more convenient to respect the essential verity than the imagination of the thing (and many have framed imaginary commonwealths and governments to themselves which never were seen nor had any real existence), for the present manner of living is so different from the way that ought to be taken, that he who neglects what is done to follow what ought to be done, will sooner learn how to ruin than how to preserve himself; for a tender man, and one that desires to be honest in everything, must needs run a great hazard among so many of a contrary principle. Wherefore it is necessary for a prince who is willing to subsist to harden himself, and learn to be good or otherwise according to the exigence of his affairs. Laying aside, therefore, all imaginable notions of a prince, and discoursing of nothing but what is actually true, I say that all men when they are spoken of, especially princes, who are in a higher and more eminent station, are remarkable for some quality or other that makes them either honourable or contemptible. Hence it is that some are counted liberal, others miserable (according to the propriety of the Tuscan word *Misero*, for *Quaro* in our language is one that desires to acquire by rapine or any other way; *Miscro* is he that abstains too much from making use of his own), some munificent, others rapacious; some cruel, others merciful; some faithless, others precise; one poor-spirited and effeminate, another fierce and ambitious; one courteous, another haughty; one modest, another libidinous; one sincere, another cunning; one rugged and morose, another accessible and easy; one grave, another giddy; one a devout, another an atheist. No man, I am sure, will deny but that it would be an admirable thing and highly to be commended to have a prince endued with all the good qualities aforesaid; but because it is impossible to have, much less to exercise, them all by reason of the frailty and crossness of our nature, it is convenient that he be so well instructed as to know how to avoid the scandal of those vices which may deprive him of his state, and be very cautious of the rest, though their consequence be not so pernicious, but where they are unavoidable he need trouble himself the less. Again, he is not to concern himself if run under the infamy of those vices without which his dominion was not to be preserved; for if we consider things impartially we shall find some things in appearance are virtuous, and yet, if pursued, would bring certain destruction; and others, on the contrary, that are seemingly bad, which, if followed by a prince, procure his peace and security.

CHAPTER 16

Of Liberality and Parsimony

To begin, then, with the first of the above-mentioned qualities, I say, it would be advantageous to be accounted liberal; nevertheless, liberality so used as not to render you formidable does but injure you; for if it be used virtuously and as it ought to be, it will not be known, nor secure you from the imputation of its contrary. To keep up, therefore, the name of liberal amongst men, it is necessary that no kind of luxury be omitted, so that a prince of that disposition will consume his revenue in those kind of expenses, and he be obliged at last, if he would preserve that reputation, to become grievous, and a great exactor upon the people, and do whatever is practicable for the getting of money, which will cause him to be hated of his subjects and despised by everybody else when he once comes to be poor; so that offending many with his liberality and rewarding but few, he becomes sensible of the first disaster, and runs great hazard of being ruined the first time he is in danger; which, when afterwards he discovers, and desires to remedy, he runs into the other extreme, and grows as odious for his avarice. So, then, if a prince cannot exercise this virtue of liberality so as to be publicly known, without detriment to himself, he ought, if he be wise, not to dread the imputation of being covetous, for in time he shall be esteemed liberal when it is discovered that by his parsimony he has increased his revenue to a condition of defending him against any invasion, and to enterprise upon other people without oppressing of them; so that he shall be accounted noble to all from whom he takes nothing away, which are an infinite number, and near and parsimonious only to such few as he gives nothing to.

In our days we have seen no great action done but by those who were accounted miserable, the other have been always undone. Pope Julius XI made use of his bounty to get into the Chair, but, to enable himself to make war with the King of France, he never practised it after, and by his frugality he maintained several wars without any tax or imposition upon the people, his long parsimony having furnished him for his extraordinary expenses. The present King of Spain, if he had affected to be thought liberal, could never have undertaken so many great designs nor obtained so many great victories. A prince, therefore, ought not so much to concern himself (so he exacts not upon his subjects, so he be able to defend himself, so he becomes not poor and despicable, nor commits rapine upon his people) though he be accounted covetous, for that is one of those vices which fortifies his dominion. If any one objects that Cæsar by his liberality made his way to the empire, and many others upon the same score of reputation have made themselves great, I answer, that you are actually a prince, or in a fair way to be made one. In the first case, liberality is hurtful; in the second, it is necessary, and Cæsar was one of those who designed upon the empire. But when he was arrived at that dignity, if he had lived, and not retrenched his expenses, he would have ruined that empire. If any replies, many have been princes, and with their armies performed great matters, who have been reputed liberal, I rejoin that a prince spends either of his own, or his subjects', or other people's. In the first case he is to be frugal; in the second, he maybe as profuse as he pleases, and baulk no point of liberality. But that prince whose army is to be maintained with free quarter and plunder and exactions from other people, is obliged to be liberal, or his army will desert him; and well he may be prodigal of what neither belongs to him nor his subjects, as was the case with Cæsar, and Cyrus, and Alexander; for to spend upon another's stock rather adds to than subtracts from his reputation; it is spending of his own that is so mortal and pernicious. Nor is there anything that destroys itself like liberality; for in the use of it, taking away the faculty of using it, thou becomest poor and contemptible, or, to avoid that poverty, thou makest thyself odious and a tyrant; and there is nothing of so much importance to a prince to prevent as to be either contemptible or odious, both which depend much upon the prudent exercise of your liberality. Upon these considerations it is more wisdom to lie under the scandal of being miserable, which is an imputation rather infamous than odious, than to be thought liberal and run yourself into a necessity of playing the tyrant, which is infamous and odious both.

CHAPTER 17

Of Cruelty and Clemency, and whether it
is best for a Prince to be beloved or feared

To come now to the other qualities proposed, I say every prince is to desire to be esteemed rather merciful than cruel, but with great caution that his mercy be not abused; Cæsar Borgia was counted cruel, yet that cruelty reduced Romagna, united it, settled it in peace, and rendered it faithful: so that if well considered, he will appear much more merciful than the Florentines, who rather than be thought cruel suffered Pistoia to be destroyed. A prince, therefore, is not to regard the scandal of being cruel, if thereby he keeps his subjects in their allegiance and united, seeing by some few examples of justice you may be more merciful than they who by an universal exercise of pity permit several disorders to follow, which occasion rapine and murder; and the reason is, because that exorbitant mercy has an ill effect upon the whole universality, whereas particular executions extend only to particular persons. But among all princes a new prince has the hardest task to avoid the scandal of being cruel by reason of the newness of his government, and the dangers which attend it: hence Virgil in the person of Dido excused the inhospitality of her government.

Res dura, & regni novitas, me talia cogunt
Moliri, & late fines Cuslode tueri.

My new dominion and my harder fate
Constrains me to't, and I must guard my
　　　State.

Nevertheless, he is not to be too credulous of reports, too hasty in his motions, nor create fears and jealousies to himself, but so to temper his administrations with prudence and humanity that neither too much confidence may make him careless, nor too much diffidence intolerable. And from hence arises a new question, Whether it be better to be beloved than feared, or feared than beloved? It is answered, both would be convenient, but because that is hard to attain, it is better and more secure, if one must be wanting, to be feared than beloved; for in the general men are ungrateful, inconstant, hypocritical, fearful of danger, and covetous of gain; whilst they receive any benefit by you, and the danger is at a distance, they are absolutely yours, their blood, their estates, their lives and their children, as I said before, are all at your service; but when mischief is at hand, and you have present need of their help, they make no scruple to revolt; and that prince who leaves himself naked of other preparations, and relies wholly upon their professions, is sure to be ruined; for amity contracted by price, and not by the greatness and generosity of the mind, may seem a good pennyworth; yet when you have occasion to make use of it, you will find no such thing. Moreover, men do with less remorse offend against those who desire to be beloved than against those who are ambitious of being feared, and the reason is because love is fastened only by a ligament of obligation, which the ill-nature of mankind breaks upon every occasion that is presented to his profit; but fear depends upon an apprehension of punishment, which is never to be dispelled. Yet a prince is to render himself awful in such sort that, if he gains not his subjects' love, he may eschew their hatred; for to be feared and not hated are compatible enough, and he may be always in that condition if he offers no violence to their estates, nor attempts anything upon the honour of their wives, as also when he has occasion to take away any man's life, if he takes his time when the cause is manifest, and he has good matter for his justification; but above all things he is to have a care of intrenching upon their estates, for men do sooner forget the death of their father than the loss of their patrimony; besides, occasions of confiscation never fail, and he that once gives way to that humour of rapine shall never want temptation to ruin his neighbour. But, on the contrary, provocations to blood are more rare, and do sooner evaporate; but when a prince is at the head of his army, and has a multitude of soldiers to govern, then it is absolutely necessary not to value the epithet of cruel, for without that no army can be kept in unity, nor in disposition for any great act.

Among the several instances of Hannibal's great conduct, it is one that, having a vast army constituted out of several nations, and conducted to make war in an enemy's country, there never happened any sedition among them, or any mutiny against their general, either in his adversity or prosperity: which can proceed from nothing so probably as his great cruelty, which, added to his infinite virtues, rendered him both awful and terrible to his soldiers, and without that all his virtues would have signified nothing. Some writers there are, but of little consideration, who admire his great exploits and condemn the true causes of them. But to prove that his other virtues would never have carried him through, let us reflect upon Scipio, a person honourable not only in his own time, but in all history whatever; nevertheless his army mutinied in Spain, and the true cause of it was his too much gentleness and lenity, which gave his soldiers more liberty than was suitable or consistent with military discipline, Fabius Maximus upbraided him by it in the Senate, and called him corrupter of the Roman Militia; the inhabitants of Locris having been plundered and destroyed by one of Scipio's lieutenants, they were never redressed, nor the legate's insolence corrected, all proceeding from the mildness of Scipio's nature, which was so eminent in him, that a person undertaking to excuse him in the Senate, declared that there were many who knew better how to avoid doing ill themselves than to punish it in other people; which temper would doubtless in time have eclipsed the glory and reputation of Scipio, had that authority been continued in him; but receiving orders and living under the direction of the Senate, that ill quality was not only not discovered in him, but turned to his renown. I conclude, therefore, according to what I have said about being feared or beloved, that forasmuch as men do love at their own discretion, but fear at their prince's, a wise prince is obliged to lay his foundation upon that which is in his own power, not that which depends on other people, but, as I said before, with great caution that he does not make himself odious.

CHAPTER 18

How far a Prince is obliged by his Promise

How honourable it is for a prince to keep his word, and act rather with integrity than collusion, I suppose everybody understands: nevertheless, experience has shown in our times that those princes who have not pinned themselves up to that punctuality and preciseness have done great things, and by their cunning and subtilty not only circumvented, and darted the brains of those with whom they had to deal, but have overcome and been too hard for those who have been so superstitiously exact. For further explanation you must understand there are two ways of contending, by law and by force: the first is proper to men; the second to beasts; but because many times the first is insufficient, recourse must be had to the second. It belongs, therefore, to a prince to understand both, when to make use of the rational and when of the brutal way; and this is recommended to princes, though abstrusely, by ancient writers, who tell them how Achilles and several other princes were committed to the education of Chiron the Centaur, who was to keep them under his discipline, choosing them a master, half man and half beast, for no other reason but to show how necessary it is for a prince to be acquainted with both, for that one without the other will be of little duration.

Seeing, therefore, it is of such importance to a prince to take upon him the nature and disposition of a beast, of all the whole flock he ought to imitate the lion and the fox; for the lion is in danger of toils and snares, and the fox of the wolf; so that he must be a fox to find out the snares, and a lion to fright away the wolves, but they who keep wholly to the lion have no true notion of themselves. A prince, therefore, who is wise and prudent, cannot or ought not to keep his parole, when the keeping of it is to his prejudice, and the causes for which he promised removed. Were men all good this doctrine was not to be taught, but because they are wicked and not likely to be punctual with you, you are not obliged to any such strictness with them; nor was there ever any prince that wanted lawful pretence to justify his breach of promise. I might instance in many modern examples, and show how many confederations, and peaces, and promises have been broken by the infidelity of princes, and how he that best personated the fox had the better success. Nevertheless, it is of great consequence to disguise your inclination, and to play the hypocrite well; and men are so simple in their temper and so submissive to their present necessities, that he that is neat and cleanly in his collusions shall never want people to practise them upon. I cannot forbear one example which is still fresh in our memory. Alexander VI never did, nor thought of, anything but cheating, and never wanted matter to work upon; and though no man promised a thing with greater asseveration, nor confirmed it with more oaths and imprecations, and observed them less, yet understanding the world well he never miscarried.

A prince, therefore, is not obliged to have all the forementioned good qualities in reality, but it is necessary he have them in appearance; nay, I will be bold to affirm that, having them actually, and employing them upon all occasions, they are extremely prejudicial, whereas, having them only in appearance, they turn to better account; it is honourable to seem mild, and merciful, and courteous, and religious, and sincere, and indeed to be so, provided your mind be so rectified and prepared that you can act quite contrary upon occasion. And this must be premised, that a prince, especially if come but lately to the throne, cannot observe all those things exactly which make men be esteemed virtuous, being oftentimes necessitated, for the preservation of his State, to do things inhuman, uncharitable, and irreligious; and, therefore, it is convenient his mind be at his command, and flexible to all the puffs and variations of fortune; not forbearing to be good whilst it is in his choice, but knowing how to be evil when there is a necessity. A prince, then, is to have particular care that nothing falls from his mouth but what is full of the five qualities aforesaid, and that to see and to hear him he appears all goodness, integrity, humanity, and religion, which last he ought to pretend to more than ordinarily, because more men do judge by the eye than by the touch; for everybody sees but few understand; everybody sees how you appear, but few know what in reality you are, and those few dare not oppose the opinion of the multitude, who have the majesty of their prince to defend them; and in the actions of all men, especially princes, where no man has power to judge, every one looks to the end. Let a prince, therefore, do what he can to preserve his life, and continue his supremacy, the means which he uses shall be thought honourable, and be commended by everybody; because the people are always taken with the appearance and event of things, and the greatest part of the world consists of the people; those few who are wise taking place when the multitude has nothing else to rely upon. There is a prince at this time in being (but his name I shall conceal) who has nothing in his mouth but fidelity and peace; and yet had he exercised either the one or the other, they had robbed him before this both of his power and reputation.

CHAPTER 19

That Princes ought to be cautious of
becoming either odious or contemptible

And because in our discourse of the qualifications of a
prince we have hitherto spoken only of those which are
of greatest importance, we shall now speak briefly of the
rest under these general heads. That a prince make it
his business (as is partly hinted before) to avoid such
things as may make him odious or contemptible, and as
often as he does that he plays his part very well, and
shall meet no danger or inconveniences by the rest of
his vices. Nothing, as I said before, makes a prince so
insufferably odious as usurping his subjects' estates and
debauching their wives, which are two things he ought
studiously to forbear; for whilst the generality of the
world live quietly upon their estates and unprejudiced
in their honour, they live peaceably enough, and all his
contention is only with the pride and ambition of some
few persons who are many ways and with great ease to
be restrained. But a prince is contemptible when he is
counted effeminate, light, inconstant, pusillanimous, and
irresolute; and of this he ought to be as careful as of a
rock in the sea, and strive that in all his actions there
may appear magnanimity, courage, gravity, and fortitude,
desiring that in the private affairs of his subjects his

sentence and determination may be irrevocable, and himself to stand so in their opinion that none may think it possible either to delude or divert him. The prince who causes himself to be esteemed in that manner shall be highly redoubted, and if he be feared, people will not easily conspire against him, nor readily invade him, because he is known to be an excellent person and formidable to his subjects; for a prince ought to be terrible in two places—at home to his subjects, and abroad to his equals, from whom he defends himself by good arms and good allies; for, if his power be good, his friends will not be wanting, and while his affairs are fixed at home, there will be no danger from abroad, unless they be disturbed by some former conspiracy; and upon any commotion *ab extra*, if he be composed at home, has lived as I prescribe, and not deserted himself, he will be able to bear up against any impression, according to the example of Nabis the Spartan. When things are well abroad his affairs at home will be safe enough, unless they be perplexed by some secret conspiracy, against which the prince sufficiently provides if he keeps himself from being hated or despised, and the people remain satisfied of him, which is a thing very necessary, as I have largely inculcated before. And one of the best remedies a prince can use against conspiracy is to keep himself from being hated or despised by the multitude; for nobody plots but expects by the death of the prince to gratify the people, and the thought of offending them will deter him from any such enterprise, because in conspiracies the difficulties are infinite. By experience we find that many conjurations have been on foot, but few have succeeded, because no man can conspire alone, nor choose a confederate but out of those who are discontented; and no sooner shall you impart your mind to a malcontent but you give him opportunity to reconcile himself, because there is nothing he proposes to himself but he may expect from the discovery. So that the gain being certain on that side, and hazardous and uncertain on the other, he must be either an extraordinary friend to you or an implacable enemy to the prince if he does not betray you; in short, on the side of the conspirators there is nothing but fear and jealousy, and apprehension of punishment; but, on the prince's side, there is the majesty of the Government, the laws, the assistance of his friends and State, which defend him so effectually that, if the affections of the people be added to them, no man can be so rash and precipitate as to conspire; for if, before the execution of his design, the conspirator has reason to be afraid, in this case he has much more afterwards, having offended the people in the execution and left himself no refuge to fly to. Of this many examples may be produced, but I shall content myself with one which happened in the memory of our fathers, Hanibal Bentivogli, grandfather to this present Hanibal, was Prince of Bolonia, and killed by the Canneschi who conspired against him, none of his race being left behind but John, who was then in his cradle; the murder was no sooner committed but the people took arms and slew all the Canneschi, which proceeded only from the affection that the house of the Bentivogli had at that time among the populace in Bolonia, which was then so great that when Hanibal was dead, there being none of that family remaining in a capacity for the government of the State, upon information that at Florence there was a natural son of the said Bentivogli's, who till that time had passed only for the son of a smith, they sent ambassadors for him, and having conducted him honourably to that city, they gave him the Government, which he executed very well till the said John came of age. I conclude, therefore, a prince need not be much apprehensive of conspiracies whilst the people are his friends; but when they are dissatisfied, and have taken prejudice against him, there is nothing nor no person which he ought not to fear. And it has been the constant care of all wise princes and all well-governed States not to reduce the nobility to despair nor the people to discontent, which is one of the most material things a prince is to prevent. Among the best-ordered monarchies of our times France is one, in which there are many good laws and constitutions tending to the liberty and preservation of the king. The first of them is the Parliament and the authority wherewith it is vested; for he who was the founder of that monarchy, being sensible of the ambition and insolence of the nobles, and judging it convenient to have them bridled and restrained: and knowing, on the other side, the hatred of the people against the nobility, and that it proceeded from fear, being willing to secure them, to exempt the king from the displeasure of the nobles if he sided with the Commons, or from the malice of the Commons if he inclined to the nobles, he erected a third judge, which, without any reflection upon the king, should keep the nobility under, and protect the people; nor could there be a better order, wiser nor of greater security to the king and the kingdom, from whence we may deduce another observation—That princes are to leave things of injustice and envy to the ministry and execution of others, but acts of favour and grace are to be performed by themselves. To conclude, a prince is to value his grandees, but so as not to make the people hate him.

Contemplating the lives and deaths of several of the Roman emperors, it is possible many would think to find plenty of examples quite contrary to my opinion, forasmuch as some of them whose conduct was remarkable, and magnanimity obvious to everybody, were turned out of their authority, or murdered by the conspiracy of their subjects. To give a punctual answer, I should inquire into the qualities and conversations of the said emperors, and in so doing I should find the reason of their ruin to be the same, or very consonant to what I have opposed. And in part I will represent such things as are most notable to the consideration of him that reads the actions of our times, and I shall content myself with the examples of all the emperors which succeeded in the empire from Marcus the philosopher to Maximinus, and they were Marcus, his son Commodus, Pertinax, Julian, Severus, Antoninus, his son Caracalla, Macrinus, Heliogabalus, Alexander, and Maximinus.

It is first to be considered that, whereas in other Governments there was nothing to contend with but the ambition of the nobles and the insolence of the people, the Roman emperors had a third inconvenience to support against the avarice and cruelty of the soldiers, which was a thing of such difficult practice that it was the occasion of the destruction of many of them, it being very uneasy to please the subject and the soldier together; for the subject loves peace, and chooses therefore a prince that is gentle and mild; whereas the soldier prefers a martial prince, and one that is haughty, and rigid, and rapacious, which good qualities they are desirous he should exercise upon the people, that their pay might be increased, and their covetousness and cruelty satiated upon them. Hence it is, that those emperors who neither by art nor nature are endued with that address and reputation as is necessary for the restraining both of the one and the other, do always miscarry; and of them the greatest part, especially if but lately advanced to the empire, understanding the inconsistency of their two humours, incline to satisfy the soldiers, without regarding how far the people are disobliged; which council is no more than is necessary; for seeing it cannot be avoided but princes must fall under the hatred of somebody, they ought diligently to contend that it be not of the multitude; if that be not to be obtained, their next great care is to be that they incur not the odium of such as are most potent among them. And, therefore, those emperors who were new, and had need of extraordinary support, adhered more readily to the soldiers than to the people, which turned to their detriment or advantage, as the prince knew how to preserve his reputation with them. From the causes aforesaid, it happened that Marcus Aurelius, Pertinax, and Alexander, being princes of more than ordinary modesty, lovers of justice, enemies of cruelty, courteous and bountiful, came all of them (except Marcus) to unfortunate ends. Marcus, indeed, lived and died in great honour, because he came to the empire by way of inheritance and succession, without being beholden either to soldiers or people, and being afterwards endued with many good qualities which recommended him, and made him venerable among them, he kept them both in such order whilst he lived, and held them so strictly to their bounds, that he was never either hated or despised. But Pertinax was chosen emperor against the will of the soldiers, who being used to live licentiously under Commodus, they could not brook that regularity to which Pertinax endeavoured to bring them; so that having contracted the odium of the soldiers, and a certain disrespect and neglect by reason of his age, he was ruined in the very beginning of his reign; from whence it is observable that hatred is obtained two ways, by good works and bad; and, therefore, a prince, as I said before, being willing to retain his jurisdiction, is oftentimes compelled to be bad. For if the chief party, whether it be people, or army, or nobility, which you think most useful and of most consequence to you for the conservation of your dignity, be corrupt, you must follow their humour and indulge them, and in that case honesty and virtue are pernicious.

But let us come to Alexander, who was a prince of such great equity and goodness, it is reckoned among his praises that in the fourteen years of his empire there was no man put to death without a fair trial; nevertheless, being accounted effeminate, and one that suffered himself to be managed by his mother, and falling by that means into disgrace, the army conspired and killed him. Examining, on the other side, the conduct of Commodus, Severus, Antoninus, Caracalla, and Maximinus, you will find them cruel and rapacious, and such as to satisfy the soldiers, omitted no kind of injury that could be exercised against the people, and all of them but Severus were unfortunate in their ends; for Severus was a prince of so great courage and magnanimity, that preserving the friendship of the army, though the people were oppressed, he made his whole reign happy, his virtues having represented him so admirable both to the soldiers and people, that these remained in a manner stupid and astonished, and the other obedient and contented. And because the actions of Severus were great in a new prince, I shall show in brief how he personated the fox and the lion, whose natures and properties are, as I said before, necessary for the imitation of a prince. Severus, therefore, knowing the laziness and inactivity of Julian the emperor, persuaded the army under his command in Sclavonia to go to Rome and revenge the death of Pertinax, who was murdered by the Imperial Guards; and under that colour, without the least pretence to the empire, he marched his army towards Rome, and was in Italy before anything of his motion was known. Being arrived at Rome, the Senate were afraid of him, killed Julian, and elected Severus. After which beginning there remained two difficulties to be removed before he could be master of the whole empire; the one was in Asia, where Niger, General of the Asiatic army, had proclaimed himself emperor; the other in the West, where Albinus the General aspired to the same. And thinking it hazardous to declare against both, he resolved to oppose himself against Niger, and cajole and wheedle Albinus, to whom he wrote word: That being chosen emperor by the Senate, he was willing to receive him to a participation of that dignity, gave him the title of Cæsar, and by consent of the Senate admitted him his colleague, which Albinus embraced very willingly, and thought him in earnest; but when Severus had overcome Niger, put him to death, and settled the affairs of the East, being returned to Rome, he complained in the Senate against Albinus as a person who, contrary to his obligations for the benefits received from him, had endeavoured treacherously to murder him; told them that he was obliged to march against him to punish his ingratitude, and afterwards following him into France, he executed his design, deprived him of his command, and put him to death. He, then, who strictly examines the actions of this prince will find him fierce as a lion, subtile as a fox, feared and reverenced by everybody, and no way odious to his army. Nor will it seem strange that he, though newly advanced to the empire, was able to defend it, seeing his great reputation protected him against the hatred which his people might have conceived against him by reason of his rapine. But his son Antoninus was an excellent person likewise endued with transcendent parts, which rendered him admirable to the people and grateful to the soldiers; for he was martial in his nature, patient of labour and hardship, and a great despiser of all sensuality and softness, which recommended him highly to his armies. Nevertheless, his fury and cruelty was so immoderately great, having upon several private and particular occasions put a great part of the people of Rome, and all the inhabitants of Alexandria, to death, that he fell into the hatred of the whole world, and began to be feared by his confidents that were about him; so that he was killed by one of his captains in the middle of his camp. From whence it may be observed, that these kind of assassinations which follow upon a deliberate and obstinate resolution, cannot be prevented by a prince; for he who values not his own life can commit them when he pleases; but they are to be feared the less, because they happen but seldom, he is only to have a care of doing any great injury to those that are about him, of which error Antoninus was too guilty, having put the brother of the said captain to an ignominious death, threatened the captain daily, and yet continued him in his guards, which was a rash and pernicious act, and proved so in the end. But to come to Commodus, who had no hard task to preserve his empire, succeeding to it by way of inheritance, as son to Marcus, for that to satisfy the people and oblige the soldiers, he had no more to do but to follow the footsteps of his father. But being of a brutish and cruel disposition, to exercise his rapacity upon the people he indulged his army, and allowed them in all manner of licentiousness. Besides prostituting his dignity by descending many times upon the theatre to fight with the gladiators, and committing many other acts which were vile and unworthy the majesty of an emperor, he became contemptible to the soldiers, and growing odious to one party and despicable to the other, they conspired and murdered him. Maximinus was likewise a martial prince, and addicted to the wars, and the army being weary of the effeminacy of Alexander, whom I have mentioned before, having slain him, they made Maximinus emperor, but he possessed it not long; for two things contributed to make him odious and despised. One was the meanness of his extraction, having kept sheep formerly in Thrace, which was known to all the world, and made him universally contemptible; the other was, that at his first coming to the empire, by not repairing immediately to Rome and putting himself into possession of his imperial seat, he had contracted the imputation of being cruel, having exercised more than ordinary severity by his prefects in Rome, and his lieutenants in all the rest of the empire; so that the whole world being provoked by the vileness of his birth and detestation of his cruelty, in apprehension of his fury, Africa, the Senate, and all the people both in Italy and Rome, conspired against him, and his own army joining themselves with them in their leaguer before Aquileia finding it difficult to be taken, weary of his cruelties, and encouraged by the multitude of his enemies, they set upon him and slew him.

I will not trouble myself with Heliogabalus, Macrinus, or Julian, who, being all effeminate and contemptible, were quickly extinguished. But I shall conclude this discourse, and say that the princes of our times are not obliged to satisfy the soldiers in their respective governments by such extraordinary ways; for though they are not altogether to be neglected, yet the remedy and resolution is easy, because none of these princes have entire armies, brought up, and inveterated in their several governments and provinces, as the armies under the Roman empire were. If, therefore, at that time it was necessary to satisfy the soldiers rather than the people, it was because the soldiers were more potent. At present it is more the interest of all princes (except the Great Turk and the Soldan) to comply with the people, because they are more considerable than the soldiers. I except the Turk, because he has in his Guards 12,000 foot and 15,000 horse constantly about him, upon whom the strength and security of his empire depends, and it is necessary (postponing all other respect to the people) they be continued his friends. It is the same case with the Soldan, who, being wholly in the power of the soldiers, it is convenient that he also waive the people and insinuate with the army. And here it is to be noted that this government of the Soldans is different from all other monarchies, for it is not unlike the Papacy in Christendom, which can neither be called a new nor an hereditary principality, because the children of the deceased prince are neither heirs to his estate nor lords of his empire, but he who is chosen to succeed by those who have the faculty of election; which custom being of old, the government cannot be called new, and by consequence is not subject to any of the difficulties wherewith a new one is infested; because, though the person of the prince be new, and perhaps the title, yet the laws and orders of State are old, and disposed to receive him as if he were hereditary lord. But to return to our business: I say that whoever considers the aforesaid discourse shall find either hatred or contempt the perpetual cause of the ruin of those emperors, and be able to judge how it came about that, part of them taking one way in their administrations and part of them another, in both parties some were happy, and some unhappy at last. Pertinax and Alexander, being but upstart princes, it was not only vain but dangerous for them to imitate Marcus, who was emperor by right of succession. Again, it was no less pernicious for Caracalla, Commodus, and Maximinus to make Severus their pattern, not having force or virtue enough to follow his footsteps. So, then, if a new prince cannot imitate the actions of Marcus, and to regulate by the example of Severus is unnecessary, he is only to take that part from Severus that is necessary to the foundation of his State, and from Marcus what is convenient to keep and defend it gloriously when it is once established and firm.

CHAPTER 20

Whether Citadels, and other things which
Princes many times do, be profitable or
dangerous

Some princes, for the greater security of their dominion,
have disarmed their subjects; others have cantonized
their countries; others have fomented factions and
animosities among them; some have applied themselves
to flatter and insinuate with those who were suspicious
in the beginning of their government; some have built
castles, others have demolished them; and though in all
these cases no certain or determined rule can be
prescribed, unless we come to a particular consideration
of the State where it is to be used, yet I shall speak of
them all, as the matter itself will endure. A wise prince,
therefore was never known to disarm his subjects; rather,
finding them unfurnished, he put arms into their hands,
for by arming them and inuring them to warlike exercise,
those arms are surely your own: they who were suspicious to you become faithful; they who are faithful are
confirmed, and all your subjects become of your party;
and because the whole multitude which submits to your
government is not capable of being armed, if you be
beneficial and obliging to those you do arm you may

make the bolder with the rest, for the difference of your behaviour to the soldier binds him more firmly to your service; and the rest will excuse you, as judging them most worthy of reward who are most liable to danger. But when you disarm you disgust them, and imply a diffidence in them, either for cowardice or treachery, and the one or the other is sufficient to give them an impression of hatred against you. And because you cannot subsist without soldiers, you will be forced to entertain mercenaries, whom I have formerly described; and if it were possible for the said mercenaries to be good, they could not be able to defend you against powerful adversaries and subjects disobliged. Wherefore, as I have said, a new prince in his new government puts his subjects always into arms, as appears by several examples in history. But when a prince conquers a new State, and annexes it, as a member to his old, then it is necessary your subjects be disarmed, all but such as appeared for you in the conquest, and they are to be mollified by degrees, and brought into such a condition of laziness and effeminacy that in time your whole strength may devolve upon your own natural militia, which were trained up in your ancient dominion and are to be always about you. Our ancestors (and they were esteemed wise men) were wont to say that it was necessary to keep Pistoia by factions and Pisa by fortresses, and accordingly, in several towns under their subjection, they created and fomented factions and animosities, to keep them with more ease. This, at a time when Italy was unsettled and in a certain kind of suspense, might be well enough done, but I do not take it at this time for any precept for us, being clearly of opinion that the making of factions never does good, but that, where the enemy approaches and the city is divided, it must necessarily, and that suddenly, be lost, because the weaker party will always fall off to the enemy, and the other cannot be able to defend it. The Venetians (as I guess) upon the same grounds nourished the factions of the Guelfs and the Ghibilins in the cities under their jurisdiction; and though they kept them from blood, yet they encouraged their dissensions, to the end that the citizens, being employed among themselves, should have no time to conspire against them; which, as appeared afterwards, did not answer expectation, for being defeated at Valia, one of the said factions took arms and turned the Venetians out of their State. Such methods, therefore, as these do argue weakness in the prince; for no government of any strength or consistence will suffer such divisions, because they are useful only in time of peace, when perhaps they may contribute to the more easy management of their subjects, but when war comes the fallacy of those counsels is quickly discovered. Without doubt, princes grow great when they overcome the difficulties and impediments which are given them; and therefore Fortune, especially when she has a mind to exalt a new prince, who has greater need of reputation than a prince that is old and hereditary, raises him up enemies and encourages enterprises against him, that he may have opportunity to conquer them, and advance himself by such steps as his enemies had prepared. For which reason many have thought that a wise prince, when opportunity offers, ought, but with great cunning and address, to maintain some enmity against himself, that when time serves to destroy them, his own greatness may be increased.

Princes, and particularly those who are not of long standing, have found more fidelity and assistance from those whom they suspected at the beginning of their reign than from those who at first were their greatest confidants. Pandolfus Petrucci, Prince of Sienna, governed his State rather by those who were suspected than others. But this is not to be treated of largely, because it varies according to the subjects. I shall only say this, that those men who in the beginning of his government opposed him, if-they be of such quality as to want the support of other people, are easily wrought over to the prince, and more strictly engaged to be faithful, because they knew that it must be their good carriage for the future that must cancel the prejudice that is against them; and so the prince comes to receive more benefit by them than by those who, serving him more securely, do most commonly neglect his affairs.

And seeing the matter requires, I will not omit to remind a prince who is but newly advanced, and that by some inward favour and correspondence in the country, that he considers well what it was that disposed those parties to befriend him; if it be not affection to him, but pique and animosity to the old government, it will cost much trouble and difficulty to keep them his friends, because it will be impossible to satisfy them; and upon serious disquisition, ancient and modern examples will give us the reason, and we shall find it more easy to gain such persons as were satisfied with the former government, and by consequence his enemies, than those who, being disobliged, sided with him and assisted to subvert it.

It has been a custom among princes, for the greater security of their territories, to build citadels and fortresses to bridle and restrain such as would enterprise against them, and to serve as a refuge in times of rebellion; and I approve the way because anciently practised, yet no longer ago than in our days, Niccolò Vitelli was known to dismantle two forts in the city of Castello, to secure his government; Guidobaldo, Duke of Urbin, returning to his State from whence Cæsar Borgia had driven him, demolished all the strong places in that province, and thereby thought it more unlikely again to fall into the hands of the enemy. The Bentivogli being returned to Bologna used the same course. So that fortresses are useful or not useful, according to the difference of time, and if in one place they do good, they do as much mischief in another. And the case may be argued thus: That prince who is more afraid of his subjects than neighbours, is to suffer them to stand; the family of the Sforzas has and will suffer more mischief by the Castle of Milan, which was built by Francesco Sforza, than by all its other troubles whatever; so that the best fortification of all is not to be hated by the people, for your fortresses will not protect you if the people have you in detestation, because they shall no sooner take arms but strangers will fall in and sustain them. In our times there is not one instance to be produced of advantage which that course has brought to any prince, but to the Countess of Furly, when, upon the death of Hieronimo, her husband, by means of those castles she was able to withstand the popular fury, and expect till supplies came to her from Milan and resettled her in the government; and as times then stood, the people were not in a condition to be relieved by any stranger, But afterwards they stood her in no stead when Cæsar Borgia invaded her, and the people, being incensed, joined with her enemy. Wherefore it had been better for her, both then and at first, to have possessed the affections of the people than all the castles in the country. These things being considered, I approve both of him that builds those fortresses and of him that neglects them, but must needs condemn him who relies so much upon them as to despise the displeasure of the people.

CHAPTER 21

How a Prince is to demean himself to gain reputation

Nothing recommends a prince so highly to the world as great enterprises and noble expressions of his own valour and conduct. We have in our days Ferdinand, King of Aragon—the present King of Spain—who may, and not improperly, be called a new prince, being of a small and weak king become for fame and renown the greatest monarch in Christendom; and if his exploits be considered you will find them all brave, but some of them extraordinary. In the beginning of his reign he invaded the kingdom of Granada, and that enterprise was the foundation of his grandeur. He began it leisurely, and without suspicion of impediment, holding the barons of Castile employed in that service, and so intent upon that war that they dreamt not of any innovation, whilst in the mean time, before they were aware, he got reputation and authority over them. He found out a way of maintaining his army at the expense of the Church and the people, and by the length of that war to establish such order and discipline among his soldiers, that afterwards they gained him many honourable victories. Besides this, to adapt him for greater enterprises (always making religion his pretence), by a kind of devout cruelty he destroyed and exterminated the Jews called Marrani, than which nothing could be more strange or deplorable. Under the same cloak of religion he invaded Africa, made his expedition into Italy, assaulted France, and began many great things which always kept the minds of his subjects in admiration and suspense, expecting what the event of his machinations would be. And these his enterprises had so sudden a spring and result one from the other that they gave no leisure to any man to be at quiet, or to continue anything against him. It is likewise of great advantage to a prince to give some rare example of his own administration at home (such is reported of Monsieur Bernardo da Milano), when there is occasion for somebody to perform anything extraordinary in the civil government, whether it be good or bad, and to find out such a way either to reward or punish him as may make him much talked of in the world. Above all, a prince is to have a care in all his actions to behave himself so as may give him the reputation of being excellent as well as great. A prince is likewise much esteemed when he shows himself a sincere friend or a generous enemy— that is, when without any hesitation he declares himself in favour of one against another, which, as it is more frank and princely, so it is more profitable than to stand neuter; for if two of your potent neighbours be at war, they are either of such condition that you are to be afraid of the victor or not; in either of which cases it will be always more for your benefit to discover yourself freely, and make a fair war. For in the first cause, if you do not declare, you shall be a prey to him who overcomes, and it will be a pleasure and satisfaction to him that is conquered to see you his fellow-sufferer; nor will anybody either defend or receive you, and the reason is, because the conqueror will never understand them to be his friends who would not assist him in his distress; and he that is worsted will not receive you because you neglected to run his fortune with your arms in your hands. Antiochus, upon the invitation of the Etolians, passed into Greece to repel the Romans. Antiochus sent ambassadors to the Achaians, who were in amity with the Romans, to persuade them to a neutrality, and the Romans sent to them to associate with them. The business coming to be debated in the Council of the Achaians, and Antiochus's ambassador pressing them to be neuters, the Roman ambassador replied: "As to what he has remonstrated, that it is most useful and most consistent with the interest of your State not to engage yourselves in our war, there is nothing more contrary and pernicious; for if you do not concern yourselves you will assuredly become a prey to the conqueror, without any thanks or reputation; and it will always be, that he who has the least kindness for you will tempt you to be neuters, but they that are your friends will invite you to take up arms." And those princes who are ill-advised, to avoid some present danger follow the neutral way, are most commonly ruined; but when a prince discovers himself courageously in favour of one party, if he with whom you join overcome, though he be very powerful, and you seem to remain at his discretion, yet he is obliged to you, and must needs have a respect for you, and men are not so wicked with such signal and exemplary ingratitude to oppress you. Besides, victories are never so clear and complete as to leave the conqueror without all sparks of reflection, and especially upon what is just. But if your confederate conies by the worst, you are received by him, and assisted whilst he is able, and becomest a companion of his fortune, which may possibly restore thee. In the second place, if they who contend be of such condition that they have no occasion to fear, let which will overcome, you are in prudence to declare yourself the sooner, because by assisting the one you contribute to the ruin of the other, whom, if your confederate had been wise, he ought rather to have preserved; so that he overcoming remains wholly at your discretion, and by your assistance he must of necessity overcome. And here it is to be noted, if he can avoid it, a prince is never to league himself with another more powerful than himself in an offensive war; because in that case if he overcomes you remain at his mercy, and princes ought to be as cautious as possible of falling under the discretion of other people. The Venetians, when there was no necessity for it, associated with France against the Duke of Milan, and that association was the cause of their ruin. But where it is not to be avoided, as happened to the Florentines when the Pope and the Spaniard sent their armies against Lombardy, there a prince is to adhere for the reasons aforesaid. Nor is any prince or government to imagine that in those cases any certain counsel can be taken, because the affairs of this world are so ordered that in avoiding one mischief we fall commonly into another. But a man's wisdom is most conspicuous where he is able to distinguish of dangers and make choice of the least; moreover, a prince to show himself a virtuoso, and honourer of ail that is excellent in any art whatsoever. He is likewise to encourage and assure his subjects that they may live quietly in peace, and exercise themselves in their several vocations, whether merchandize, agriculture, or any other employment whatever, to the end that one may not forbear improving or embellishing his estate for fear it should be taken from him, nor another advancing his trade in apprehension of taxes; but the prince is rather to excite them by propositions of reward, and immunities to all such as shall any way amplify his territory or power. He is obliged, likewise, at convenient times in the year to entertain the people by feastings and plays, and spectacles of recreation; and, because all cities are divided into companies or wards, he ought to have respect to those societies, be merry with them sometimes, and give them some instance of his humanity and magnificence, but always retaining the majesty of his degree, which is never to be debased in any case whatever.

CHAPTER 22

Of the Secretaries of Princes

The election of his ministers is of no small importance to a prince, for the first judgment that is made of him or his parts is from the persons he has about him. When they are wise and faithful, be sure the prince is discreet himself, who, as he knew how to choose them able at first, so he has known how to oblige them to be faithful; but, when his ministers are otherwise, it reflects shrewdly upon the prince, for commonly the first error he commits is in the election of his servants. No man knew Antonia da Venafro to be secretary to Pandolfo Petrucci, Prince of Sienna, but he could judge Pandolfo to be a prudent man for choosing such a one as his minister, In the capacities and parts of men there are three sorts of degrees: one man understands of himself, another understands what is explained, and a third understands neither of himself nor by any explanation. The first is excellent, the second commendable, the third altogether unprofitable, If, therefore, Pandolfo was not in the first rank, he might be included in the second; for whenever a prince has the judgment to know the good and the bad of what is spoken or done, though his own invention be not excellent, he can distinguish a good servant from a bad, and exalt the one and correct the other; and the minister, despairing of deluding him, remains good in spite of his teeth. But the business is, how a prince may understand his minister, and the rule for that is infallible. When you observe your officer more careful of himself than of you, and all his actions and designs pointing at his own interest and advantage, that man will never be a good minister, nor ought you ever to repose any confidence in him; for he who has the affairs of his prince in his hand ought to lay aside all thoughts of himself, and regard nothing but what is for the profit of his master. And, on the other side, to keep him faithful, the prince is as much concerned to do for him, by honouring him, enriching him, giving him good offices and preferments, that the wealth and honour conferred by his master may keep him from looking out for himself, and the plenty and goodness of his offices make him afraid of a change, knowing that without his prince's favour he can never subsist. When, therefore, the prince and the minister are qualified in this manner they may depend one upon the other; but when it is otherwise with them the end must be bad, and one of them will be undone.

CHAPTER 23

How Flatterers are to be avoided

I will not pass by a thing of great consequence, being an error against which princes do hardly defend themselves, unless they be very wise and their judgment very good; and that is about flatterers, of which kind of cattle all histories are full; for men are generally so fond of their own actions, and so easily mistaken in them, that it is not without difficulty they defend themselves against those sort of people, and he that goes about to defend himself runs a great hazard of being despised; for there is no other remedy against flatterers than to let everybody understand you are not disobliged by telling the truth; yet if you suffer everybody to tell it you injure yourself and lessen your reverence. Wherefore a wise prince ought to go a third way, and select out of his State certain discreet men, to whom only he is to commit that liberty of speaking truth, and that of such things as he demands, and nothing else; but then he is to inquire of everything, hear their opinions, and resolve afterwards, as he pleases, and behave himself towards them in such sort that every one may find with how much the more freedom he speaks, with so much the more kindness he is accepted; that besides them he will hearken to nobody; that he considers well before he resolves; and that his resolutions, once taken, are never to be altered. He that does otherwise shall either precipitate his affairs by means of his flatterers, or by variety of advices often change his designs, which will lessen his esteem and render him contemptible. To this purpose I shall instance in one modern example.

Father Lucas, a servant to Maximilian, the present emperor, giving a character of his Majesty, declared him a person who never consulted anybody, and yet never acted according to his own judgment and inclination; and the reason was because he proceeded contrary to the prescriptions aforesaid—for the emperor is a close man, communicates his secrets to nobody, nor takes any man's advice; but when his determinations are to be executed and begin to be known in the world, those who are about him begin to discourage and dissuade him, and he, being good-natured, does presently desist. Hence it comes to pass that his resolutions of one day are dissolved in the next; no man knows what he desires or designs, nor no man can depend upon his resolutions. A prince, therefore, is always to consult, but at his own, not other people's pleasure, and rather to deter people from giving their advice undemanded; but he ought not to be sparing in his demands, nor when he has demanded, impatient of hearing the truth; but if he understands that any suppressed it and forbore to speak out for fear of displeasing, then, and not till then, he is to show his displeasure. And because there are those who believe that a prince which creates an opinion of his prudence in the people, does it not by any excellence in his own nature, but by the counsels of those who are about him, without doubt they are deceived; for this is a general and infallible rule—That that prince who has no wisdom of his own can never be well advised, unless by accident he commits all to the government and administration of some honest and discreet man. In this case it is possible things may be well ordered for awhile, but they can never continue, for his minister or vicegerent in a short time will set up for himself; but if a prince who has no great judgment of his own con suits with more than one, their counsels will never agree, nor he have ever the cunning to unite them. Every man will advise according to his own interest or caprice, and he not have the parts either to correct or discover it; and other counsellors are not to be found, for men will always prove bad, unless by necessity they are compelled to be good. So then it is clear—That good counsels, from whomsoever they come, proceed rather from the wisdom of the prince than the prince's wisdom from the goodness of his counsels.

CHAPTER 24

How it came to pass that the Princes of
Italy have most of them lost their
dominions

The qualities aforesaid being observed, they make a new
prince appear in the number of the more ancient, and
render him presently more firm and secure in his
government than if he had descended to it by right of
inheritance; for the actions of a new prince are liable to
stricter observation than if he were hereditary, and when
they are known to be virtuous gain more upon people and
oblige them further than antiquity of blood; because men
are more affected with present than past things, and when
in their present condition they find themselves well, they
content themselves with it, without looking out anywhere
else, employing themselves wholly in defence of their
prince, unless in other things he be defective to himself;
so that thereby he will have double honour in having laid
the foundation of a new principality, and embellished and
fortified it with good laws, good force, good friends, and
good example; whereas he multiplies his disgrace, who,
being born prince, loses his inheritance by his own ill-
management and imprudence. And if the sovereign princes
in Italy, who in our time have lost their dominions, be

considered, as the King of Naples, the Duke of Milan, and others, there will be found in their beginning one common defect as to the management of their arms, for the reasons largely discoursed of before; besides, some of them will appear to have been hated by the people, or if they have had so much prudence as to preserve a friendship with them, they have been ignorant how to secure themselves against the grandees; for without these errors no States are lost that have money and strength enough to bring an army into the field. Philip of Macedon (not Alexander the Great's father, but he who was overcome by Titus Quintus) had no great force in comparison of the Romans and the Grecians which invaded him; yet, being a martial man, and one that understood how to insinuate with the people and oblige the nobility, he maintained war several years against both of them, and though at last he lost some towns, yet he kept his kingdom in spite of them. Those, therefore, of our princes who for many years together were settled in their principalities, if they lost them afterwards, they cannot accuse fortune, but their own negligence and indiscretion for not having in quiet times considered they might change (and it is the common infirmity of mankind in a calm to make no reckoning of a tempest) when adversity approached; they thought more of making their escape than defence, resting their whole hopes upon this, that when the people were weary of the insolence of the conqueror, they would recall them again; which resolution is tolerable indeed when others are wanting, but to neglect all other remedies and trust only to that, is much to be condemned, for a man would never throw himself down that another might take him up; besides, that may not happen, or if it does, not with your security, because that kind of defence is poor and depends not on yourself, and no defences are good, certain, and lasting, which proceed not from the prince's own courage and virtue.

CHAPTER 25

How far in human affairs Fortune may
avail, and in what manner she may be
resisted

I am not ignorant that it is, and has been of old the
opinion of many people, that the affairs of the world are
so governed by fortune and Divine Providence that man
cannot by his wisdom correct them, or apply any remedy
at all; from whence they would infer that we are not to
labour and sweat, but to leave everything to its own
tendency and event. This opinion has obtained more in
our days by the many and frequent revolutions which
have been and are still seen beyond all human conjecture.
And, when I think of it seriously sometimes, I am in
some measure inclined to it myself; nevertheless, that
our own free will may not utterly be exploded, I conceive
it may be true that fortune may have the arbitrament of
one-half of our actions, but that she leaves the other
half, or little less, to be governed by ourselves. Fortune
I do resemble to a rapid and impetuous river, which
when swelled and enraged overwhelms the plains,
subverts the trees and the houses, forces away the earth
from one place and carries it to another; everybody fears,
everybody shuns, but nobody knows how to resist it; yet

though it be thus furious sometimes, it does not follow but when it is quiet and calm men may by banks and fences, and other provisions, correct it in such manner that when it swells again it may be carried off by some canal, or the violence thereof rendered less licentious and destructive. So it is with fortune, which shows her power where there is no predisposed virtue to resist it, and turns all her force and impetuosity where she knows there are no banks, no fences to restrain her. If you consider Italy (the scat of all these revolutions), and what it was that caused them, you will find it an open field, without any bounds or ramparts to secure it; and that, had it been defended by the courage of their ancestors, as Germany and Spain and France have been, those inundations had never happened, or never made such devastation as they have done. And this I hold sufficient to have spoken in general against fortune. But restraining myself a little more to particulars, I say it is ordinary to see a prince happy one day and ruined the next, without discerning any difference in his humour or government; and this I impute to the reasons of which I have discoursed largely before; and one of them is, because that prince which relies wholly upon fortune, being subject to her variations, must of necessity be ruined. I believe, again, that prince may be happy whose manner of proceeding concerts with the times, and he unhappy who cannot accommodate to them; for in things leading to the end of their designs (which every man has in his eye, and they are riches and honour), we see men have various methods of proceeding. Some with circumspection, others with heat; some with violence, others with cunning; some with patience, and others with fury; and every one, notwithstanding the diversity of their ways, may possibly attain them. Again, we see two persons equally cautious, one of them prospers, and the other miscarries; and on the other side, two equally happy by different measures, one being deliberate, and the other as hasty; and this proceeds from nothing but the condition of the times, which suits or does not suit with the manner of their proceedings. From hence arises what I have said, that two persons by different operations do attain the same end, whilst two others steer the same course, and one of them succeeds and the other is ruined. From hence, likewise, may be reduced the vicissitudes of good; for if to one who manages with deliberation and patience, the times and conjuncture of affairs come about so favourably that his conduct be in fashion, he must needs be happy; but if the face of affairs and the times change, and he changes not with them, he is certainly ruined. Nor is there any man to be found so wise that knows how to accommodate or frame himself to all these varieties, both because he cannot deviate from that to which Nature has inclined him; as likewise because, if a man has constantly prospered in one way, it is no easy matter to persuade him to another; and he that is so cautious, being at a loss when time requires he should be vigorous, must of necessity be destroyed; whereas, if he could turn with the times, his fortune would never betray him. Pope Julius XI in all his enterprises acted with passion and vehemence, and the times and accident of affairs were so suitable to his manner of proceeding that he prospered in whatever he undertook. Consider his expedition of Bolonia in the days of Monsieur Giovanni Bentivogli; the Venetians were against it, and the Kings of Spain and France were in treaty, and had a mind to it themselves; yet he with his promptitude and fury undertook it personally himself, and that activity of his kept both Spaniard and Venetian in suspense (the Venetians for fear, the Spaniards in hopes to recover the whole kingdom of Naples), and the King of France came over to his side; for seeing him in motion, and desirous to make him his friend, and thereby to correct the insolence of the Venetian, he thought he could not deny him his assistance without manifest injustice; so that Julius with his rashness and huffing did that which never any other Pope could have done with all his cunning and insinuation, for had he deferred his departure from Rome till all things had been put into exact order, and his whole progress concluded, as any other Pope would have done, he could never have succeeded; the king of France would have pretended a thousand excuses, and others would have suggested twice as many fears. I will pass by the rest of his enterprises, which were all alike and prospered as well, and the shortness of his life secured him against change; for had the times fallen out so that he had been forced to proceed with accurate circumspection, he would have certainly been ruined, for he could never have left those ways to which his nature inclined him. I conclude, then, that whilst the obstinacy of princes consists with the motion of fortune, it is possible they may be happy; but when once they disagree, the poor prince comes certainly to the ground. I am of opinion, likewise, that it is better to be hot and precipitate than cautious and apprehensive; for fortune is a woman, and must be hectored to keep her under; and it is visible every day she suffers herself to be managed by those who are brisk and audacious rather than by those who are cold and phlegmatic in their motions, and therefore, like a woman, she is always a friend to those who are young, because being less circumspect they attack her with more security and boldness.

CHAPTER 26

An Exhortation to deliver Italy from the Barbarians

Having weighed, therefore, all that is said before, and considered seriously with myself whether in this juncture of affairs in Italy the times were disposed for the advancement of a new prince, and whether there was competent matter that could give occasion to a virtuous and wise person to introduce such a form as would bring reputation to him and benefit to all his subjects, it seems to me that at this present so many things concur to the exaltation of a new prince that I do not know any time that has been more proper than this; and if, as I said before, for the manifestation of the courage of Moses it was necessary that the Israelites should be captives in Egypt; for discovery of the magnanimity of Cyrus, that the Persians should be oppressed by the Medes; and for the illustration of the excellence of Theseus that the Athenians should be banished and dispersed; so to evince and demonstrate the courage of an Italian spirit it was necessary that Italy should be reduced to its present condition; that it should be in greater bondage than the Jews, in greater servitude than the Persians, and in greater dispersion than the Athenians; without head, without order, harassed, spoiled, overcome, overrun, and overflown with all kind of calamity; and though formerly some sparks of virtue have appeared in some persons that might give it hopes that God had ordained them for its redemption, yet it was found afterwards that in the very height and career of their exploits they were checked and forsaken by fortune, and poor Italy left half dead, expecting who would be her Samaritan to bind up her wounds, put an end to the sackings and devastations in Lombardy, the taxes and expilations in the kingdom of Naples and Tuscany, and cure her sores which length of time had festered and imposthumated. It is manifest how she prays to God daily to send some person who may redeem her from the cruelty and insolence of the barbarians. It is manifest how prone and ready she is to follow the banner that any man will take up; nor is it at present to be discerned where she can repose her hopes with more probability than in your illustrious family, which by its own courage and interest and the favour of God and the Church (of which it is now chief), may be induced to make itself head in her redemption; which will be no hard matter to be effected if you lay before you the lives and actions of the persons above-named; who though they were rare and wonderful were yet but men, and not accommodated with so fair circumstances as you. Their enterprise was not more just nor easy, nor God Almighty more their friend than yours. You have justice on your side; for that war is just which is necessary, and it is piety to fight where no hope is left in anything else. The people are universally disposed, and where the disposition is so great the opposition can be but small, especially you taking your rules from those persons which I have proposed to you for a model. Besides, many things that they did were supernatural, and by God's immediate conduct the sea opened, a cloud directed, a rock afforded water, it rained manna, all these things are recompensed in your grandeur, and the rest remains to be executed by you. God will not do everything immediately, because He will not deprive us of our free will and the honour that devolves upon us. Nor is it any wonder if none of the aforenamed Italians have been able to do that which may be hoped for from your illustrious family; and if in so many revolutions in Italy, and so long continuation of war, their military virtue seems spent and extinguished, the reason is, their old discipline was not good, and nobody was able to direct a better. Nothing makes so much to the honour of a new prince as new laws and new orders invented by him, which, if they be well founded, and carry anything of grandeur along with them, do render him venerable and wonderful; and Italy is susceptible enough of any new form. Their courage is great enough in the soldier if it be not wanting in the officer; witness the duels and combats, in which the Italians have generally the better by their force and dexterity and stratagem; but come to their battles, and they have oftener the worst, and all from the inexperience of their commanders; for those who pretend to have skill will never obey, and every one thinks he has skill, there having been nobody to this very day raised by his virtue and fortune to that height of reputation as to prevail with others to obey him. Hence it came that, in so long time, in the many wars during the last twenty years, whenever an army consisted wholly of Italians it was certainly beaten; and this may be testified by Tarus, Alexandria, Capua, Genoa, Vaila, Bologna, and Mestri. If, therefore, your illustrious family be inclined to follow the examples of those excellent persons who redeemed their countries, it is necessary, as a true fundamental of all great enterprises, to provide yourselves with forces of your own subjects, for you cannot have more faithful nor better soldiers than they. And though all of them be good, yet altogether they will be much better when they find themselves not only commanded but preferred and caressed by a prince of their own. It is necessary, therefore, to be furnished with these forces before you can be able with Italian virtue to vindicate your country from the oppression of strangers. And though the Swiss and Spanish infantry be counted terrible, they have both of them their defects; and a third sort may be composed that may not only encounter but be confident to beat them; for the Spanish foot cannot deal with horse, and the Swiss are not invincible when they meet with foot as obstinate as themselves. It has been seen by experience, and would be so again, the Spaniards cannot sustain the fury of the French cavalry, and the Swiss have been overthrown by the infantry of Spain. And though of this last we have seen no perfect experiment, yet we had a competent essay at the battle of Ravenna, where the Spanish foot being engaged with the German battalions (which observe the same order and discipline with the Swiss), the Spaniards, by the agility of their bodies and the protection of their bucklers, broke in tinder their pikes and killed them securely, while the poor Germans were incapable to defend themselves; and had not the Spaniards been charged by the horse, the German foot had been certainly cut off. It is possible, therefore, the defect of both those foot being known, to institute a third which may buckle with the horse and be in no fear of their foot; which will be effected not by the variation of their arms but by changing their discipline, And these are some of those things which, being newly reformed, give great grandeur and reputation to any new prince. This opportunity, therefore, is by no means to be slipped, that Italy, after so long expectation, may see some hopes of deliverance. Nor can it be expressed with what joy, with what impatience of revenge, with what fidelity, with what compassion, with what tears such a champion would be received into all the provinces that have suffered by those barbarous inundations. What gates would be shut against him? What people would deny him obedience? What malice would oppose him? What true Italian would refuse to follow him? There is not, there is not anybody but abhors and nauseates this barbarous domination. Let your illustrious family, then, address itself to the work with as much courage and confidence as just enterprises are undertaken; that under their ensigns our country may be recovered, and under their conduct Petrarch's prophecy may be fulfilled, who has promised that—

> *Virtù contra furore*
> *Prenderà l'arme, e fic'l combatter corto:*
> *Che l'antico valore*
> *Negl'Italici cor non è ancor morto.*

> Virtue shall arm 'gainst rage, and in short
>   fight
> Prove the *Roman* valour's not extinguish'd
>   quite.

CLASSIC LITERATURE: WORDS AND PHRASES
adapted from the Collins English Dictionary

Accoucheur NOUN a male midwife or doctor ❑ *I think my sister must have had some general idea that I was a young offender whom an Accoucheur Policemen had taken up (on my birthday) and delivered over to her* (*Great Expectations* by Charles Dickens)

addled ADJ confused and unable to think properly ❑ *But she counted and counted till she got that addled* (*The Adventures of Huckleberry Finn* by Mark Twain)

admiration NOUN amazement or wonder ❑ *lifting up his hands and eyes by way of admiration* (*Gulliver's Travels* by Jonathan Swift)

afeard ADJ afeard means afraid ❑ *shake it – and don't be afeard* (*The Adventures of Huckleberry Finn* by Mark Twain)

affected VERB affected means followed ❑ *Hadst thou affected sweet divinity* (*Doctor Faustus 5.2* by Christopher Marlowe)

aground ADV when a boat runs aground, it touches the ground in a shallow part of the water and gets stuck ❑ *what kep' you? – boat get aground?* (*The Adventures of Huckleberry Finn* by Mark Twain)

ague NOUN a fever in which the patient has alternate hot and cold shivering fits ❑ *his exposure to the wet and cold had brought on fever and ague* (*Oliver Twist* by Charles Dickens)

alchemy ADJ false or worthless ❑ *all wealth alchemy* (*The Sun Rising* by John Donne)

all alike PHRASE the same all the time ❑ *Love, all alike* (*The Sun Rising* by John Donne)

alow and aloft PHRASE alow means in the lower part or bottom, and aloft means on the top, so alow and aloft means on the top and in the bottom or throughout ❑ *Someone's turned the chest out alow and aloft* (*Treasure Island* by Robert Louis Stevenson)

ambuscade NOUN ambuscade is not a proper word. Tom means an ambush, which is when a group of people attack their enemies, after hiding and waiting for them ❑ *and so we would lie in ambuscade, as he called it* (*The Adventures of Huckleberry Finn* by Mark Twain)

amiable ADJ likeable or pleasant ❑ *Such amiable qualities must speak for themselves* (*Pride and Prejudice* by Jane Austen)

amulet NOUN an amulet is a charm thought to drive away evil spirits. ❑ *uttered phrases at once occult and familiar, like the amulet worn on the heart* (*Silas Marner* by George Eliot)

amusement NOUN here amusement means a strange and disturbing puzzle ❑ *this was an amusement the other way* (*Robinson Crusoe* by Daniel Defoe)

ancient NOUN an ancient was the flag displayed on a ship to show which country it belongs to. It is also called the ensign ❑ *her ancient and pendants out* (*Robinson Crusoe* by Daniel Defoe)

antic ADJ here antic means horrible or grotesque ❑ *armed and dressed after a very antic manner* (*Gulliver's Travels* by Jonathan Swift)

antics NOUN antics is an old word meaning clowns, or people who do silly things to make other people laugh ❑ *And point like antics at his triple crown* (*Doctor Faustus 3.2* by Christopher Marlowe)

appanage NOUN an appanage is a living allowance ❑ *As if loveliness were not the special prerogative of woman – her legitimate appanage and heritage!* (*Jane Eyre* by Charlotte Brontë)

appended VERB appended means attached or added to ❑ *and these words appended* (*Treasure Island* by Robert Louis Stevenson)

approver NOUN an approver is someone who gives evidence against someone he used to work with ❑ *Mr. Noah Claypole: receiving a free pardon from the Crown in consequence of being admitted approver against Fagin* (*Oliver Twist* by Charles Dickens)

areas NOUN the areas is the space, below street level, in front of the basement of a house ❑ *The Dodger had a vicious propensity, too, of pulling the caps from the heads of small boys and tossing them down areas* (*Oliver Twist* by Charles Dickens)

argument NOUN theme or important idea or subject which runs through a piece of writing ❑ *Thrice needful to the argument which now* (*The Prelude* by William Wordsworth) .

artificially ADJ artfully or cleverly ❑ *and he with a sharp flint sharpened very artificially* (*Gulliver's Travels* by Jonathan Swift)

artist NOUN here artist means a skilled workman ❑ *This man was a most ingenious artist* (*Gulliver's Travels* by Jonathan Swift)

assizes NOUN assizes were regular court sessions which a visiting judge was in charge of ❑ *you shall hang at the next assizes* (*Treasure Island* by Robert Louis Stevenson)

attraction NOUN gravitation, or Newton's theory of gravitation ❑ *he predicted the same fate to attraction* (*Gulliver's Travels* by Jonathan Swift)

aver VERB to aver is to claim something strongly ❑ *for Jem Rodney,*

the mole catcher, averred that one evening as he was returning homeward (*Silas Marner* by George Eliot)

baby NOUN here baby means doll, which is a child's toy that looks like a small person ❑ *and skilful dressing her baby* (*Gulliver's Travels* by Jonathan Swift)

bagatelle NOUN bagatelle is a game rather like billiards and pool ❑ *Breakfast had been ordered at a pleasant little tavern, a mile or so away upon the rising ground beyond the green; and there was a bagatelle board in the room, in case we should desire to unbend our minds after the solemnity.* (*Great Expectations* by Charles Dickens)

bah EXCLAM Bah is an exclamation of frustration or anger ❑ *"Bah," said Scrooge.* (*A Christmas Carol* by Charles Dickens)

bairn NOUN a northern word for child ❑ *Who has taught you those fine words, my bairn?* (*Wuthering Heights* by Emily Brontë)

bait VERB to bait means to stop on a journey to take refreshment ❑ *So, when they stopped to bait the horse, and ate and drank and enjoyed themselves, I could touch nothing that they touched, but kept my fast unbroken.* (*David Copperfield* by Charles Dickens)

balustrade NOUN a balustrade is a row of vertical columns that form railings ❑ *but I mean to say you might have got a hearse up that staircase, and taken it broadwise, with the splinter-bar towards the wall, and the door towards the balustrades: and done it easy* (*A Christmas Carol* by Charles Dickens)

bandbox NOUN a large lightweight box for carrying bonnets or hats ❑ *I am glad I bought my bonnet, if it is only for the fun of having another bandbox* (*Pride and Prejudice* by Jane Austen)

barren NOUN a barren here is a stretch or expanse of barren land ❑ *a line* *of upright stones, continued the length of the barren* (*Wuthering Heights* by Emily Brontë)

basin NOUN a basin was a cup without a handle ❑ *who is drinking his tea out of a basin* (*Wuthering Heights* by Emily Brontë)

battalia NOUN the order of battle ❑ *till I saw part of his army in battalia* (*Gulliver's Travels* by Jonathan Swift)

battery NOUN a Battery is a fort or a place where guns are positioned ❑ *You bring the lot to me, at that old Battery over yonder* (*Great Expectations* by Charles Dickens)

battledore and shuttlecock NOUN The game battledore and shuttlecock was an early version of the game now known as badminton. The aim of the early game was simply to keep the shuttlecock from hitting the ground. ❑ *Battledore and shuttlecock's a wery good game vhen you an't the shuttlecock and two lawyers the battledores, in which case it gets too excitin' to be pleasant* (*Pickwick Papers* by Charles Dickens)

beadle NOUN a beadle was a local official who had power over the poor ❑ *But these impertinences were speedily checked by the evidence of the surgeon, and the testimony of the beadle* (*Oliver Twist* by Charles Dickens)

bearings NOUN the bearings of a place are the measurements or directions that are used to find or locate it ❑ *the bearings of the island* (*Treasure Island* by Robert Louis Stevenson)

beaufet NOUN a beaufet was a sideboard ❑ *and sweet-cake from the beaufet* (*Emma* by Jane Austen)

beck NOUN a beck is a small stream ❑ *a beck which follows the bend of the glen* (*Wuthering Heights* by Emily Brontë)

bedight VERB decorated ❑ *and bedight with Christmas holly stuck into the top.* (*A Christmas Carol* by Charles Dickens)

Bedlam NOUN Bedlam was a lunatic asylum in London which had statues carved by Caius Gabriel Cibber at its entrance ❑ *Bedlam, and those carved maniacs at the gates* (*The Prelude* by William Wordsworth)

beeves NOUN oxen or castrated bulls which are animals used for pulling vehicles or carrying things ❑ *to deliver in every morning six beeves* (*Gulliver's Travels* by Jonathan Swift)

begot VERB created or caused ❑ *Begot in thee* (*On His Mistress* by John Donne)

behoof NOUN behoof means benefit ❑ *"Yes, young man," said he, releasing the handle of the article in question, retiring a step or two from my table, and speaking for the behoof of the landlord and waiter at the door* (*Great Expectations* by Charles Dickens)

berth NOUN a berth is a bed on a boat ❑ *this is the berth for me* (*Treasure Island* by Robert Louis Stevenson)

bevers NOUN a bever was a snack, or small portion of food, eaten between main meals ❑ *that buys me thirty meals a day and ten bevers* (*Doctor Faustus 2.1* by Christopher Marlowe)

bilge water NOUN the bilge is the widest part of a ship's bottom, and the bilge water is the dirty water that collects there ❑ *no gush of bilge-water had turned it to fetid puddle* (*Jane Eyre* by Charlotte Brontë)

bills NOUN bills is an old term meaning prescription. A prescription is the piece of paper on which your doctor writes an order for medicine and which you give to a chemist to get the medicine ❑ *Are not thy bills hung up as monuments* (*Doctor Faustus 1.1* by Christopher Marlowe)

black cap NOUN a judge wore a black cap when he was about to sentence a prisoner to death ❑ *The judge* assumed the black cap, and the prisoner still stood with the same air and gesture. (*Oliver Twist* by Charles Dickens)

black gentleman NOUN this was another word for the devil ❑ *for she is as impatient as the black gentleman* (*Emma* by Jane Austen)

boot-jack NOUN a wooden device to help take boots off ❑ *The speaker appeared to throw a boot-jack, or some such article, at the person he addressed* (*Oliver Twist* by Charles Dickens)

booty NOUN booty means treasure or prizes ❑ *would be inclined to give up their booty in payment of the dead man's debts* (*Treasure Island* by Robert Louis Stevenson)

Bow Street runner PHRASE Bow Street runners were the first British police force, set up by the author Henry Fielding in the eighteenth century ❑ *as would have convinced a judge or a Bow Street runner* (*Treasure Island* by Robert Louis Stevenson)

brawn NOUN brawn is a dish of meat which is set in jelly ❑ *Heaped up upon the floor, to form a kind of throne, were turkeys, geese, game, poultry, brawn, great joints of meat, sucking-pigs* (*A Christmas Carol* by Charles Dickens)

bray VERB when a donkey brays, it makes a loud, harsh sound ❑ *and she doesn't bray like a jackass* (*The Adventures of Huckleberry Finn* by Mark Twain)

break VERB in order to train a horse you first have to break it ❑ *"If a high-mettled creature like this," said he, "can't be broken by fair means, she will never be good for anything"* (*Black Beauty* by Anna Sewell)

bullyragging VERB bullyragging is an old word which means bullying. To bullyrag someone is to threaten or force someone to do something they don't want to do ❑ *and a lot of loafers bullyragging him for sport* (*The Adventures of Huckleberry Finn* by Mark Twain)

but PREP except for (this) ❑ *but this, all pleasures fancies be* (*The Good-Morrow* by John Donne)

by hand PHRASE by hand was a common expression of the time meaning that baby had been fed either using a spoon or a bottle rather than by breast-feeding ❑ *My sister, Mrs. Joe Gargery, was more than twenty years older than I, and had established a great reputation with herself . . . because she had bought me up 'by hand'* (*Great Expectations* by Charles Dickens)

bye-spots NOUN bye-spots are lonely places ❑ *and bye-spots of tales rich with indigenous produce* (*The Prelude* by William Wordsworth)

calico NOUN calico is plain white fabric made from cotton ❑ *There was two old dirty calico dresses* (*The Adventures of Huckleberry Finn* by Mark Twain)

camp-fever NOUN camp-fever was another word for the disease typhus ❑ *during a severe camp-fever* (*Emma* by Jane Austen)

cant NOUN cant is insincere or empty talk ❑ *"Man," said the Ghost, "if man you be in heart, not adamant, forbear that wicked cant until you have discovered What the surplus is, and Where it is."* (*A Christmas Carol* by Charles Dickens)

canty ADJ canty means lively, full of life ❑ *My mother lived til eighty, a canty dame to the last* (*Wuthering Heights* by Emily Brontë)

canvas VERB to canvas is to discuss ❑ *We think so very differently on this point Mr Knightley, that there can be no use in canvassing it* (*Emma* by Jane Austen)

capital ADJ capital means excellent or extremely good ❑ *for it's capital, so shady, light, and big* (*Little Women* by Louisa May Alcott)

capstan NOUN a capstan is a device used on a ship to lift sails and anchors ❑ *capstans going, ships going out to sea, and unintelligible sea creatures* roaring curses over the bulwarks at respondent lightermen (*Great Expectations* by Charles Dickens)

case-bottle NOUN a square bottle designed to fit with others into a case ❑ *The spirit being set before him in a huge case-bottle, which had originally come out of some ship's locker* (*The Old Curiosity Shop* by Charles Dickens)

casement NOUN casement is a word meaning window. The teacher in Nicholas Nickleby misspells window showing what a bad teacher he is ❑ *W-i-n, win, d-e-r, der, winder, a casement.'* (*Nicholas Nickleby* by Charles Dickens)

cataleptic ADJ a cataleptic fit is one in which the victim goes into a trance-like state and remains still for a long time ❑ *It was at this point in their history that Silas's cataleptic fit occurred during the prayer-meeting* (*Silas Marner* by George Eliot)

cauldron NOUN a cauldron is a large cooking pot made of metal ❑ *stirring a large cauldron which seemed to be full of soup* (*Alice's Adventures in Wonderland* by Lewis Carroll)

cephalic ADJ cephalic means to do with the head ❑ *with ink composed of a cephalic tincture* (*Gulliver's Travels* by Jonathan Swift)

chaise and four NOUN a closed four-wheel carriage pulled by four horses ❑ *he came down on Monday in a chaise and four to see the place* (*Pride and Prejudice* by Jane Austen)

chamberlain NOUN the main servant in a household ❑ *In those times a bed was always to be got there at any hour of the night, and the chamberlain, letting me in at his ready wicket, lighted the candle next in order on his shelf* (*Great Expectations* by Charles Dickens)

characters NOUN distinguishing marks ❑ *Impressed upon all forms the characters* (*The Prelude* by William Wordsworth)

chary ADJ cautious ❑ *I should have been chary of discussing my guardian too freely even with her* (*Great Expectations* by Charles Dickens)

cherishes VERB here cherishes means cheers or brightens ❑ *some philosophic song of Truth that cherishes our daily life* (*The Prelude* by William Wordsworth)

chickens' meat PHRASE chickens' meat is an old term which means chickens' feed or food ❑ *I had shook a bag of chickens' meat out in that place* (*Robinson Crusoe* by Daniel Defoe)

chimeras NOUN a chimera is an unrealistic idea or a wish which is unlikely to be fulfilled ❑ *with many other wild impossible chimeras* (*Gulliver's Travels* by Jonathan Swift)

chines NOUN chine is a cut of meat that includes part or all of the backbone of the animal ❑ *and they found hams and chines uncut* (*Silas Marner* by George Eliot)

chits NOUN chits is a slang word which means girls ❑ *I hate affected, niminy-piminy chits!* (*Little Women* by Louisa May Alcott)

chopped VERB chopped means come suddenly or accidentally ❑ *if I had chopped upon them* (*Robinson Crusoe* by Daniel Defoe)

chute NOUN a narrow channel ❑ *One morning about day-break, I found a canoe and crossed over a chute to the main shore* (*The Adventures of Huckleberry Finn* by Mark Twain)

circumspection NOUN careful observation of events and circumstances; caution ❑ *I honour your circumspection* (*Pride and Prejudice* by Jane Austen)

clambered VERB clambered means to climb somewhere with difficulty, usually using your hands and your feet ❑ *he clambered up and down stairs* (*Treasure Island* by Robert Louis Stevenson)

clime NOUN climate ❑ *no season knows nor clime* (*The Sun Rising* by John Donne)

clinched VERB clenched ❑ *the tops whereof I could but just reach with my fist clinched* (*Gulliver's Travels* by Jonathan Swift)

close chair NOUN a close chair is a sedan chair, which is an covered chair which has room for one person. The sedan chair is carried on two poles by two men, one in front and one behind ❑ *persuaded even the Empress herself to let me hold her in her close chair* (*Gulliver's Travels* by Jonathan Swift)

clown NOUN clown here means peasant or person who lives off the land ❑ *In ancient days by emperor and clown* (*Ode on a Nightingale* by John Keats)

coalheaver NOUN a coalheaver loaded coal onto ships using a spade ❑ *Good, strong, wholesome medicine, as was given with great success to two Irish labourers and a coalheaver* (*Oliver Twist* by Charles Dickens)

coal-whippers NOUN men who worked at docks using machines to load coal onto ships ❑ *here, were colliers by the score and score, with the coal-whippers plunging off stages on deck* (*Great Expectations* by Charles Dickens)

cobweb NOUN a cobweb is the net which a spider makes for catching insects ❑ *the walls and ceilings were all hung round with cobwebs* (*Gulliver's Travels* by Jonathan Swift)

coddling VERB coddling means to treat someone too kindly or protect them too much ❑ *and I've been coddling the fellow as if I'd been his grandmother* (*Little Women* by Louisa May Alcott)

coil NOUN coil means noise or fuss or disturbance ❑ *What a coil is there?* (*Doctor Faustus 4.7* by Christopher Marlowe)

collared VERB to collar something is a slang term which means to capture.

In this sentence, it means he stole it [the money] ❑ *he collared it* (*The Adventures of Huckleberry Finn* by Mark Twain)

colling VERB colling is an old word which means to embrace and kiss ❑ *and no clasping and colling at all* (*Tess of the D'Urbervilles* by Thomas Hardy)

colloquies NOUN colloquy is a formal conversation or dialogue ❑ *Such colloquies have occupied many a pair of pale-faced weavers* (*Silas Marner* by George Eliot)

comfit NOUN sugar-covered pieces of fruit or nut eaten as sweets ❑ *and pulled out a box of comfits* (*Alice's Adventures in Wonderland* by Lewis Carroll)

coming out VERB when a girl came out in society it meant she was of marriageable age. In order to 'come out' girls were expecting to attend balls and other parties during a season ❑ *The younger girls formed hopes of coming out a year or two sooner than they might otherwise have done* (*Pride and Prejudice* by Jane Austen)

commit VERB commit means arrest or stop ❑ *Commit the rascals* (*Doctor Faustus 4.7* by Christopher Marlowe)

commodious ADJ commodious means convenient ❑ *the most commodious and effectual ways* (*Gulliver's Travels* by Jonathan Swift)

commons NOUN commons is an old term meaning food shared with others ❑ *his pauper assistants ranged themselves behind him; the gruel was served out; and a long grace was said over the short commons.* (*Oliver Twist* by Charles Dickens)

complacency NOUN here complacency means a desire to please others. Today complacency means feeling pleased with oneself without good reason. ❑ *Twas thy power that raised the first complacency in me* (*The Prelude* by William Wordsworth)

complaisance NOUN complaisance was eagerness to please ❑ *we cannot wonder at his complaisance* (Pride and Prejudice by Jane Austen)

complaisant ADJ complaisant means polite ❑ *extremely cheerful and complaisant to their guest* (Gulliver's Travels by Jonathan Swift)

conning VERB conning means learning by heart ❑ *Or conning more* (The Prelude by William Wordsworth)

consequent NOUN consequence ❑ *as avarice is the necessary consequent of old age* (Gulliver's Travels by Jonathan Swift)

consorts NOUN concerts ❑ *The King, who delighted in music, had frequent consorts at Court* (Gulliver's Travels by Jonathan Swift)

conversible ADJ conversible meant easy to talk to, companionable ❑ *He can be a conversible companion* (Pride and Prejudice by Jane Austen)

copper NOUN a copper is a large pot that can be heated directly over a fire ❑ *He gazed in stupefied astonishment on the small rebel for some seconds, and then clung for support to the copper* (Oliver Twist by Charles Dickens)

copper-stick NOUN a copper-stick is the long piece of wood used to stir washing in the copper (or boiler) which was usually the biggest cooking pot in the house ❑ *It was Christmas Eve, and I had to stir the pudding for next day, with a copper-stick, from seven to eight by the Dutch clock* (Great Expectations by Charles Dickens)

counting-house NOUN a counting house is a place where accountants work ❑ *Once upon a time – of all the good days in the year, on Christmas Eve – old Scrooge sat busy in his countinghouse* (A Christmas Carol by Charles Dickens)

courtier NOUN a courtier is someone who attends the king or queen – a member of the court ❑ *next the ten courtiers;* (Alice's Adventures in Wonderland by Lewis Carroll)

covies NOUN covies were flocks of partridges ❑ *and will save all of the best covies for you* (Pride and Prejudice by Jane Austen)

cowed VERB cowed means frightened or intimidated ❑ *it cowed me more than the pain* (Treasure Island by Robert Louis Stevenson)

cozened VERB cozened means tricked or deceived ❑ *Do you remember, sir, how you cozened me* (Doctor Faustus 4.7 by Christopher Marlowe)

cravats NOUN a cravat is a folded cloth that a man wears wrapped around his neck as a decorative item of clothing ❑ *we'd a' slept in our cravats to-night* (The Adventures of Huckleberry Finn by Mark Twain)

crock and dirt PHRASE crock and dirt is an old expression meaning soot and dirt ❑ *and the mare catching cold at the door, and the boy grimed with crock and dirt* (Great Expectations by Charles Dickens)

crockery NOUN here crockery means pottery ❑ *By one of the parrots was a cat made of crockery* (The Adventures of Huckleberry Finn by Mark Twain)

crooked sixpence PHRASE it was considered unlucky to have a bent sixpence ❑ *You've got the beauty, you see, and I've got the luck, so you must keep me by you for your crooked sixpence* (Silas Marner by George Eliot)

croquet NOUN croquet is a traditional English summer game in which players try to hit wooden balls through hoops ❑ *and once she remembered trying to box her own ears for having cheated herself in a game of croquet* (Alice's Adventures in Wonderland by Lewis Carroll)

cross PREP across ❑ *The two great streets, which run cross and divide it into four quarters* (Gulliver's Travels by Jonathan Swift)

culpable ADJ if you are culpable for something it means you are to blame ❑ *deep are the sorrows that spring from false ideas for which no man is culpable.* (*Silas Marner* by George Eliot)

cultured ADJ cultivated ❑ *Nor less when spring had warmed the cultured Vale* (*The Prelude* by William Wordsworth)

cupidity NOUN cupidity is greed ❑ *These people hated me with the hatred of cupidity and disappointment.* (*Great Expectations* by Charles Dickens)

curricle NOUN an open two-wheeled carriage with one seat for the driver and space for a single passenger ❑ *and they saw a lady and a gentleman in a curricle* (*Pride and Prejudice* by Jane Austen)

cynosure NOUN a cynosure is something that strongly attracts attention or admiration ❑ *Then I thought of Eliza and Georgiana; I beheld one the cynosure of a ballroom, the other the inmate of a convent cell* (*Jane Eyre* by Charlotte Brontë)

dalliance NOUN someone's dalliance with something is a brief involvement with it ❑ *nor sporting in the dalliance of love* (*Doctor Faustus Chorus* by Christopher Marlowe)

darkling ADV darkling is an archaic way of saying in the dark ❑ *Darkling I listen* (*Ode on a Nightingale* by John Keats)

delf-case NOUN a sideboard for holding dishes and crockery ❑ *at the pewter dishes and delf-case* (*Wuthering Heights* by Emily Brontë)

determined ■ VERB here determined means ended ❑ *and be out of vogue when that was determined* (*Gulliver's Travels* by Jonathan Swift) ■ VERB determined can mean to have been learned or found especially by investigation or experience ❑ *All the sensitive feelings it wounded so cruelly, all the shame and misery it kept alive within my breast, became more poignant as I thought of this; and I determined that the life was unendurable* (*David Copperfield* by Charles Dickens)

Deuce NOUN a slang term for the Devil ❑ *Ah, I dare say I did. Deuce take me, he added suddenly, I know I did. I find I am not quite unscrewed yet.* (*Great Expectations* by Charles Dickens)

diabolical ADJ diabolical means devilish or evil ❑ *and with a thousand diabolical expressions* (*Treasure Island* by Robert Louis Stevenson)

direction NOUN here direction means address ❑ *Elizabeth was not surprised at it, as Jane had written the direction remarkably ill* (*Pride and Prejudice* by Jane Austen)

discover VERB to make known or announce ❑ *the Emperor would discover the secret while I was out of his power* (*Gulliver's Travels* by Jonathan Swift)

dissemble VERB hide or conceal ❑ *Dissemble nothing* (*On His Mistress* by John Donne)

dissolve VERB dissolve here means to release from life, to die ❑ *Fade far away, dissolve, and quite forget* (*Ode on a Nightingale* by John Keats)

distrain VERB to distrain is to seize the property of someone who is in debt in compensation for the money owed ❑ *for he's threatening to distrain for it* (*Silas Marner* by George Eliot)

Divan NOUN a Divan was originally a Turkish council of state – the name was transferred to the couches they sat on and is used to mean this in English ❑ *Mr Brass applauded this picture very much, and the bed being soft and comfortable, Mr Quilp determined to use it, both as a sleeping place by night and as a kind of Divan by day.* (*The Old Curiosity Shop* by Charles Dickens)

divorcement NOUN separation ❑ *By all pains which want and* *divorcement hath* (*On His Mistress* by John Donne)

dog in the manger, PHRASE this phrase describes someone who prevents you from enjoying something that they themselves have no need for ❑ *You are a dog in the manger, Cathy, and desire no one to be loved but yourself* (*Wuthering Heights* by Emily Brontë)

dolorifuge NOUN dolorifuge is a word which Thomas Hardy invented. It means pain-killer or comfort ❑ *as a species of dolorifuge* (*Tess of the D'Urbervilles* by Thomas Hardy)

dome NOUN building ❑ *that river and that mouldering dome* (*The Prelude* by William Wordsworth)

domestic PHRASE here domestic means a person's management of the house ❑ *to give some account of my domestic* (*Gulliver's Travels* by Jonathan Swift)

dunce NOUN a dunce is another word for idiot ❑ *Do you take me for a dunce? Go on?* (*Alice's Adventures in Wonderland* by Lewis Carroll)

Ecod EXCLAM a slang exclamation meaning 'oh God!' ❑ *"Ecod," replied Wemmick, shaking his head, "that's not my trade."* (*Great Expectations* by Charles Dickens)

egg-hot NOUN an egg-hot (see also 'flip' and 'negus') was a hot drink made from beer and eggs, sweetened with nutmeg ❑ *She fainted when she saw me return, and made a little jug of egg-hot afterwards to console us while we talked it over.* (*David Copperfield* by Charles Dickens)

encores NOUN an encore is a short extra performance at the end of a longer one, which the entertainer gives because the audience has enthusiastically asked for it ❑ *we want a little something to answer encores with, anyway* (*The Adventures of Huckleberry Finn* by Mark Twain)

equipage NOUN an elegant and impressive carriage ❑ *and besides, the equipage did not answer to any of*

their neighbours (*Pride and Prejudice* by Jane Austen)

exordium NOUN an exordium is the opening part of a speech ❑ *"Now, Handel," as if it were the grave beginning of a portentous business exordium, he had suddenly given up that tone* (*Great Expectations* by Charles Dickens)

expect VERB here expect means to wait for ❑ *to expect his farther commands* (*Gulliver's Travels* by Jonathan Swift)

familiars NOUN familiars means spirits or devils who come to someone when they are called ❑ *I'll turn all the lice about thee into familiars* (*Doctor Faustus 1.4* by Christopher Marlowe)

fantods NOUN a fantod is a person who fidgets or can't stop moving nervously ❑ *It most give me the fantods* (*The Adventures of Huckleberry Finn* by Mark Twain)

farthing NOUN a farthing is an old unit of British currency which was worth a quarter of a penny ❑ *Not a farthing less. A great many back-payments are included in it, I assure you.* (*A Christmas Carol* by Charles Dickens)

farthingale NOUN a hoop worn under a skirt to extend it ❑ *A bell with an old voice – which I dare say in its time had often said to the house, Here is the green farthingale* (*Great Expectations* by Charles Dickens)

favours NOUN here favours is an old word which means ribbons ❑ *A group of humble mourners entered the gate: wearing white favours* (*Oliver Twist* by Charles Dickens)

feigned VERB pretend or pretending ❑ *not my feigned page* (*On His Mistress* by John Donne)

fence ■ NOUN a fence is someone who receives and sells stolen goods ❑ *What are you up to? Ill-treating the boys, you covetous, avaricious, in-sa-ti-a-ble old fence?* (*Oliver Twist* by

Charles Dickens) ■ NOUN defence or protection □ *but honesty hath no fence against superior cunning* (*Gulliver's Travels* by Jonathan Swift)

fess ADJ fess is an old word which means pleased or proud □ *You'll be fess enough, my poppet* (*Tess of the D'Urbervilles* by Thomas Hardy)

fettered ADJ fettered means bound in chains or chained □ *"You are fettered," said Scrooge, trembling. "Tell me why?"* (*A Christmas Carol* by Charles Dickens)

fidges VERB fidges means fidgets, which is to keep moving your hands slightly because you are nervous or excited □ *Look, Jim, how my fingers fidges* (*Treasure Island* by Robert Louis Stevenson)

finger-post NOUN a finger-post is a sign-post showing the direction to different places □ *"The gallows," continued Fagin, "the gallows, my dear, is an ugly finger-post, which points out a very short and sharp turning that has stopped many a bold fellow's career on the broad highway."* (*Oliver Twist* by Charles Dickens)

fire-irons NOUN fire-irons are tools kept by the side of the fire to either cook with or look after the fire □ *the fire-irons came first* (*Alice's Adventures in Wonderland* by Lewis Carroll)

fire-plug NOUN a fire-plug is another word for a fire hydrant □ *The pony looked with great attention into a fire-plug, which was near him, and appeared to be quite absorbed in contemplating it* (*The Old Curiosity Shop* by Charles Dickens)

flank NOUN flank is the side of an animal □ *And all her silken flanks with garlands dressed* (*Ode on a Grecian Urn* by John Keats)

flip NOUN a flip is a drink made from warmed ale, sugar, spice and beaten egg □ *The events of the day, in combination with the twins, if not with the flip, had made Mrs. Micawber hysterical, and she shed tears as she replied* (*David Copperfield* by Charles Dickens)

flit VERB flit means to move quickly □ *and if he had meant to flit to Thrushcross Grange* (*Wuthering Heights* by Emily Brontë)

floorcloth NOUN a floorcloth was a hard-wearing piece of canvas used instead of carpet □ *This avenging phantom was ordered to be on duty at eight on Tuesday morning in the hall (it was two feet square, as charged for floorcloth)* (*Great Expectations* by Charles Dickens)

fly-driver NOUN a fly-driver is a carriage drawn by a single horse □ *The fly-drivers, among whom I inquired next, were equally jocose and equally disrespectful* (*David Copperfield* by Charles Dickens)

fob NOUN a small pocket in which a watch is kept □ *"Certain," replied the man, drawing a gold watch from his fob* (*Oliver Twist* by Charles Dickens)

folly NOUN folly means foolishness or stupidity □ *the folly of beginning a work* (*Robinson Crusoe* by Daniel Defoe)

fond ADJ fond means foolish □ *Fond worldling* (*Doctor Faustus 5.2* by Christopher Marlowe)

fondness NOUN silly or foolish affection □ *They have no fondness for their colts or foals* (*Gulliver's Travels* by Jonathan Swift)

for his fancy PHRASE for his fancy means for his liking or as he wanted □ *and as I did not obey quick enough for his fancy* (*Treasure Island* by Robert Louis Stevenson)

forlorn ADJ lost or very upset □ *you are from that day forlorn* (*Gulliver's Travels* by Jonathan Swift)

foster-sister NOUN a foster-sister was someone brought up by the same nurse or in the same household □ *I had been his foster-sister* (*Wuthering Heights* by Emily Brontë)

fox-fire NOUN fox-fire is a weak glow that is given off by decaying, rotten wood □ *what we must have was a lot of them rotten chunks* that's called fox-fire (*The Adventures of Huckleberry Finn* by Mark Twain)

frozen sea PHRASE the Arctic Ocean ❑ *into the frozen sea* (*Gulliver's Travels* by Jonathan Swift)

gainsay VERB to gainsay something is to say it isn't true or to deny it ❑ *"So she had," cried Scrooge. "You're right. I'll not gainsay it, Spirit. God forbid!"* (*A Christmas Carol* by Charles Dickens)

gaiters NOUN gaiters were leggings made of a cloth or piece of leather which covered the leg from the knee to the ankle ❑ *Mr Knightley was hard at work upon the lower buttons of his thick leather gaiters* (*Emma* by Jane Austen)

galluses NOUN galluses is an old spelling of gallows, and here means suspenders. Suspenders are straps worn over someone's shoulders and fastened to their trousers to prevent the trousers falling down ❑ *and home-knit galluses* (*The Adventures of Huckleberry Finn* by Mark Twain)

galoot NOUN a sailor but also a clumsy person ❑ *and maybe a galoot on it chopping* (*The Adventures of Huckleberry Finn* by Mark Twain)

gayest ADJ gayest means the most lively and bright or merry ❑ *Beth played her gayest march* (*Little Women* by Louisa May Alcott)

gem NOUN here gem means jewellery ❑ *the mountain shook off turf and flower, had only heath for raiment and crag for gem* (*Jane Eyre* by Charlotte Brontë)

giddy ADJ giddy means dizzy ❑ *and I wish you wouldn't keep appearing and vanishing so suddenly; you make me quite giddy.* (*Alice's Adventures in Wonderland* by Lewis Carroll)

gig NOUN a light two-wheeled carriage ❑ *when a gig drove up to the garden gate: out of which there jumped a fat gentleman* (*Oliver Twist* by Charles Dickens)

gladsome ADJ gladsome is an old word meaning glad or happy ❑ *Nobody ever stopped him in the street to say, with gladsome looks* (*A Christmas Carol* by Charles Dickens)

glen NOUN a glen is a small valley; the word is used commonly in Scotland ❑ *a beck which follows the bend of the glen* (*Wuthering Heights* by Emily Brontë)

gravelled VERB gravelled is an old term which means to baffle or defeat someone ❑ *Gravelled the pastors of the German Church* (*Doctor Faustus 1.1* by Christopher Marlowe)

grinder NOUN a grinder was a private tutor ❑ *but that when he had had the happiness of marrying Mrs Pocket very early in his life, he had impaired his prospects and taken up the calling of a Grinder* (*Great Expectations* by Charles Dickens)

gruel NOUN gruel is a thin, watery corn-meal or oatmeal soup ❑ *and the little saucepan of gruel (Scrooge had a cold in his head) upon the hob.* (*A Christmas Carol* by Charles Dickens)

guinea, half a NOUN a half guinea was ten shillings and sixpence ❑ *but lay out half a guinea at Ford's* (*Emma* by Jane Austen)

gull VERB gull is an old term which means to fool or deceive someone ❑ *Hush, I'll gull him supernaturally* (*Doctor Faustus 3.4* by Christopher Marlowe)

gunnel NOUN the gunnel, or gunwhale, is the upper edge of a boat's side ❑ *But he put his foot on the gunnel and rocked her* (*The Adventures of Huckleberry Finn* by Mark Twain)

gunwale NOUN the side of a ship ❑ *He dipped his hand in the water over the boat's gunwale* (*Great Expectations* by Charles Dickens)

Gytrash NOUN a Gytrash is an omen of misfortune to the superstitious, usually taking the form of a hound ❑ *I remembered certain of Bessie's tales, wherein figured a*

North-of-England spirit, called a 'Gytrash' (*Jane Eyre* by Charlotte Brontë)

hackney-cabriolet NOUN a two-wheeled carriage with four seats for hire and pulled by a horse ❑ *A hackney-cabriolet was in waiting; with the same vehemence which she had exhibited in addressing Oliver, the girl pulled him in with her, and drew the curtains close.* (*Oliver Twist* by Charles Dickens)

hackney-coach NOUN a four-wheeled horse-drawn vehicle for hire ❑ *The twilight was beginning to close in, when Mr. Brownlow alighted from a hackney-coach at his own door, and knocked softly.* (*Oliver Twist* by Charles Dickens)

haggler NOUN a haggler is someone who travels from place to place selling small goods and items ❑ *when I be plain Jack Durbeyfield, the haggler* (*Tess of the D'Urbervilles* by Thomas Hardy)

halter NOUN a halter is a rope or strap used to lead an animal or to tie it up ❑ *I had of course long been used to a halter and a headstall* (*Black Beauty* by Anna Sewell)

hamlet NOUN a hamlet is a small village or a group of houses in the countryside ❑ *down from the hamlet* (*Treasure Island* by Robert Louis Stevenson)

hand-barrow NOUN a hand-barrow is a device for carrying heavy objects. It is like a wheelbarrow except that it has handles, rather than wheels, for moving the barrow ❑ *his sea chest following behind him in a hand-barrow* (*Treasure Island* by Robert Louis Stevenson)

handspike NOUN a handspike was a stick which was used as a lever ❑ *a bit of stick like a handspike* (*Treasure Island* by Robert Louis Stevenson)

haply ADV haply means by chance or perhaps ❑ *And haply the Queen-Moon is on her throne* (*Ode on a Nightingale* by John Keats)

harem NOUN the harem was the part of the house where the women lived ❑ *mostly they hang round the harem* (*The Adventures of Huckleberry Finn* by Mark Twain)

hautboys NOUN hautboys are oboes ❑ *sausages and puddings resembling flutes and hautboys* (*Gulliver's Travels* by Jonathan Swift)

hawker NOUN a hawker is someone who sells goods to people as he travels rather than from a fixed place like a shop ❑ *to buy some stockings from a hawker* (*Treasure Island* by Robert Louis Stevenson)

hawser NOUN a hawser is a rope used to tie up or tow a ship or boat ❑ *Again among the tiers of shipping, in and out, avoiding rusty chain-cables, frayed hempen hawsers* (*Great Expectations* by Charles Dickens)

headstall NOUN the headstall is the part of the bridle or halter that goes around a horse's head ❑ *I had of course long been used to a halter and a headstall* (*Black Beauty* by Anna Sewell)

hearken VERB hearken means to listen ❑ *though we sometimes stopped to lay hold of each other and hearken* (*Treasure Island* by Robert Louis Stevenson)

heartless ADJ here heartless means without heart or dejected ❑ *I am not heartless* (*The Prelude* by William Wordsworth)

hebdomadal ADJ hebdomadal means weekly ❑ *It was the hebdomadal treat to which we all looked forward from Sabbath to Sabbath* (*Jane Eyre* by Charlotte Brontë)

highwaymen NOUN highwaymen were people who stopped travellers and robbed them ❑ *We are highwaymen* (*The Adventures of Huckleberry Finn* by Mark Twain)

hinds NOUN hinds means farm hands, or people who work on a farm ❑ *He called his hinds about him* (*Gulliver's Travels* by Jonathan Swift)

histrionic ADJ if you refer to someone's behaviour as histrionic, you are being critical of it because it is dramatic and exaggerated ❑ *But the histrionic muse is the darling* (*The Adventures of Huckleberry Finn* by Mark Twain)

hogs NOUN hogs is another word for pigs ❑ *Tom called the hogs 'ingots'* (*The Adventures of Huckleberry Finn* by Mark Twain)

horrors NOUN the horrors are a fit, called delirium tremens, which is caused by drinking too much alcohol ❑ *I'll have the horrors* (*Treasure Island* by Robert Louis Stevenson)

huffy ADJ huffy means to be obviously annoyed or offended about something ❑ *They will feel that more than angry speeches or huffy actions* (*Little Women* by Louisa May Alcott)

hulks NOUN hulks were prison-ships ❑ *The miserable companion of thieves and ruffians, the fallen outcast of low haunts, the associate of the scourings of the jails and hulks* (*Oliver Twist* by Charles Dickens)

humbug NOUN humbug means nonsense or rubbish ❑ *"Bah," said Scrooge. "Humbug!"* (*A Christmas Carol* by Charles Dickens)

humours NOUN it was believed that there were four fluids in the body called humours which decided the temperament of a person depending on how much of each fluid was present ❑ *other peccant humours* (*Gulliver's Travels* by Jonathan Swift)

husbandry NOUN husbandry is farming animals ❑ *bad husbandry were plentifully anointing their wheels* (*Silas Marner* by George Eliot)

huswife NOUN a huswife was a small sewing kit ❑ *but I had put my huswife on it* (*Emma* by Jane Austen)

ideal ADJ ideal in this context means imaginary ❑ *I discovered the yell was not ideal* (*Wuthering Heights* by Emily Brontë)

If our two PHRASE if both our ❑ *If our two loves be one* (*The Good-Morrow* by John Donne)

ignis-fatuus NOUN ignis-fatuus is the light given out by burning marsh gases, which lead careless travellers into danger ❑ *it is madness in all women to let a secret love kindle within them, which, if unreturned and unknown, must devour the life that feeds it; and, if discovered and responded to, must lead ignis-fatuus-like, into miry wilds whence there is no extrication.* (*Jane Eyre* by Charlotte Brontë)

imaginations NOUN here imaginations means schemes or plans ❑ *soon drove out those imaginations* (*Gulliver's Travels* by Jonathan Swift)

impressible ADJ impressible means open or impressionable ❑ *for Marner had one of those impressible, self-doubting natures* (*Silas Marner* by George Eliot)

in good intelligence PHRASE friendly with each other ❑ *that these two persons were in good intelligence with each other* (*Gulliver's Travels* by Jonathan Swift)

inanity NOUN inanity is sillyness or dull stupidity ❑ *Do we not wile away moments of inanity* (*Silas Marner* by George Eliot)

incivility NOUN incivility means rudeness or impoliteness ❑ *if it's only for a piece of incivility like to-night's* (*Treasure Island* by Robert Louis Stevenson)

indigenae NOUN indigenae means natives or people from that area ❑ *an exotic that the surly indigenae will not recognise for kin* (*Wuthering Heights* by Emily Brontë)

indocible ADJ unteachable ❑ *so they were the most restive and indocible* (*Gulliver's Travels* by Jonathan Swift)

ingenuity NOUN inventiveness ❑ *entreated me to give him something as an encouragement to ingenuity*

(*Gulliver's Travels* by Jonathan Swift)

ingots NOUN an ingot is a lump of a valuable metal like gold, usually shaped like a brick ❑ *Tom called the hogs 'ingots'* (*The Adventures of Huckleberry Finn* by Mark Twain)

inkstand NOUN an inkstand is a pot which was put on a desk to contain either ink or pencils and pens ❑ *throwing an inkstand at the Lizard as she spoke* (*Alice's Adventures in Wonderland* by Lewis Carroll)

inordinate ADJ without order. Today inordinate means 'excessive'. ❑ *Though yet untutored and inordinate* (*The Prelude* by William Wordsworth)

intellectuals NOUN here intellectuals means the minds (of the workmen) ❑ *those instructions they give being too refined for the intellectuals of their workmen* (*Gulliver's Travels* by Jonathan Swift)

interview NOUN meeting ❑ *By our first strange and fatal interview* (*On His Mistress* by John Donne)

jacks NOUN jacks are rods for turning a spit over a fire ❑ *It was a small bit of pork suspended from the kettle hanger by a string passed through a large door key, in a way known to primitive housekeepers unpossessed of jacks* (*Silas Marner* by George Eliot)

jews-harp NOUN a jews-harp is a small, metal, musical instrument that is played by the mouth ❑ *A jews-harp's plenty good enough for a rat* (*The Adventures of Huckleberry Finn* by Mark Twain)

jorum NOUN a large bowl ❑ *while Miss Skiffins brewed such a jorum of tea, that the pig in the back premises became strongly excited* (*Great Expectations* by Charles Dickens)

jostled VERB jostled means bumped or pushed by someone or some people ❑ *being jostled himself into the kennel* (*Gulliver's Travels* by Jonathan Swift)

keepsake NOUN a keepsake is a gift which reminds someone of an event or of the person who gave it to them. ❑ *books and ornaments they had in their boudoirs at home: keepsakes that different relations had presented to them* (*Jane Eyre* by Charlotte Brontë)

kenned VERB kenned means knew ❑ *though little kenned the lamplighter that he had any company but Christmas!* (*A Christmas Carol* by Charles Dickens)

kennel NOUN kennel means gutter, which is the edge of a road next to the pavement, where rain water collects and flows away ❑ *being jostled himself into the kennel* (*Gulliver's Travels* by Jonathan Swift)

knock-knee ADJ knock-knee means slanted, at an angle. ❑ *LOT 1 was marked in whitewashed knock-knee letters on the brewhouse* (*Great Expectations* by Charles Dickens)

ladylike ADJ to be ladylike is to behave in a polite, dignified and graceful way ❑ *No, winking isn't ladylike* (*Little Women* by Louisa May Alcott)

lapse NOUN flow ❑ *Stealing with silent lapse to join the brook* (*The Prelude* by William Wordsworth)

larry NOUN larry is an old word which means commotion or noisy celebration ❑ *That was all a part of the larry!* (*Tess of the D'Urbervilles* by Thomas Hardy)

laths NOUN laths are strips of wood ❑ *The panels shrunk, the windows cracked; fragments of plaster fell out of the ceiling, and the naked laths were shown instead* (*A Christmas Carol* by Charles Dickens)

leer NOUN a leer is an unpleasant smile ❑ *with a kind of leer* (*Treasure Island* by Robert Louis Stevenson)

lenitives NOUN these are different kinds of drugs or medicines: lenitives and palliatives were pain relievers; aperitives were laxatives;

abstersives caused vomiting; corrosives destroyed human tissue; restringents caused constipation; cephalalgics stopped headaches; icterics were used as medicine for jaundice; apophlegmatics were cough medicine, and acoustics were cures for the loss of hearing ❑ *lenitives, aperitives, abstersives, corrosives, restringents, palliatives, laxatives, cephalalgics, icterics, apophlegmatics, acoustics* (Gulliver's Travels by Jonathan Swift)

lest CONJ in case. If you do something lest something (usually) unpleasant happens you do it to try to prevent it happening ❑ *She went in without knocking, and hurried upstairs, in great fear lest she should meet the real Mary Ann* (Alice's Adventures in Wonderland by Lewis Carroll)

levee NOUN a levee is an old term for a meeting held in the morning, shortly after the person holding the meeting has got out of bed ❑ *I used to attend the King's levee once or twice a week* (Gulliver's Travels by Jonathan Swift)

life-preserver NOUN a club which had lead inside it to make it heavier and therefore more dangerous ❑ *and with no more suspicious articles displayed to view than two or three heavy bludgeons which stood in a corner, and a 'life-preserver' that hung over the chimney-piece.* (Oliver Twist by Charles Dickens)

lighterman NOUN a lighterman is another word for sailor ❑ *in and out, hammers going in ship-builders' yards, saws going at timber, clashing engines going at things unknown, pumps going in leaky ships, capstans going, ships going out to sea, and unintelligible sea creatures roaring curses over the bulwarks at respondent lightermen* (Great Expectations by Charles Dickens)

livery NOUN servants often wore a uniform known as a livery ❑ *suddenly a footman in livery came running out of the wood* (Alice's Adventures in Wonderland by Lewis Carroll)

livid ADJ livid means pale or ash coloured. Livid also means very angry ❑ *a dirty, livid white* (Treasure Island by Robert Louis Stevenson)

lottery-tickets NOUN a popular card game ❑ *and Mrs. Philips protested that they would have a nice comfortable noisy game of lottery tickets* (Pride and Prejudice by Jane Austen)

lower and upper world PHRASE the earth and the heavens are the lower and upper worlds ❑ *the changes in the lower and upper world* (Gulliver's Travels by Jonathan Swift)

lustres NOUN lustres are chandeliers. A chandelier is a large, decorative frame which holds light bulbs or candles and hangs from the ceiling ❑ *the lustres, lights, the carving and the guilding* (The Prelude by William Wordsworth)

lynched VERB killed without a criminal trial by a crowd of people ❑ *He'll never know how nigh he come to getting lynched* (The Adventures of Huckleberry Finn by Mark Twain)

malingering VERB if someone is malingering they are pretending to be ill to avoid working ❑ *And you stand there malingering* (Treasure Island by Robert Louis Stevenson)

managing PHRASE treating with consideration ❑ *to think the honour of my own kind not worth managing* (Gulliver's Travels by Jonathan Swift)

manhood PHRASE manhood means human nature ❑ *concerning the nature of manhood* (Gulliver's Travels by Jonathan Swift)

man-trap NOUN a man-trap is a set of steel jaws that snap shut when trodden on and trap a person's leg ❑ *"Don't go to him," I called out of the window, "he's an assassin! A*

man-trap!" (*Oliver Twist* by
Charles Dickens)

maps NOUN charts of the night sky ❑
*Let maps to others, worlds on worlds
have shown* (*The Good-Morrow* by
John Donne)

mark VERB look at or notice ❑ *Mark
but this flea, and mark in this* (*The
Flea* by John Donne)

maroons NOUN A maroon is someone
who has been left in a place which
it is difficult for them to escape
from, like a small island ❑ *if schooners, islands, and maroons* (*Treasure
Island* by Robert Louis Stevenson)

mast NOUN here mast means the fruit
of forest trees ❑ *a quantity of
acorns, dates, chestnuts, and other
mast* (*Gulliver's Travels* by Jonathan
Swift)

mate VERB defeat ❑ *Where Mars did
mate the warlike Carthigens* (*Doctor
Faustus Chorus* by Christopher
Marlowe)

mealy ADJ Mealy when used to
describe a face meant palid, pale or
colourless ❑ *I only know two sorts
of boys. Mealy boys, and beef-faced
boys* (*Oliver Twist* by Charles
Dickens)

middling ADJ fairly or moderately
❑ *she worked me middling hard for
about an hour* (*The Adventures of
Huckleberry Finn* by Mark Twain)

mill NOUN a mill, or treadmill, was a
device for hard labour or punishment in prison ❑ *Was you never on
the mill?* (*Oliver Twist* by Charles
Dickens)

milliner's shop NOUN a milliner's sold
fabrics, clothing, lace and accesso-
ries; as time went on they specialized
more and more in hats ❑ *to pay
their duty to their aunt and to a
milliner's shop just over the way*
(*Pride and Prejudice* by Jane
Austen)

minching un' munching PHRASE how
people in the north of England
used to describe the way people
from the south speak ❑ *Minching*

un' munching! (*Wuthering Heights*
by Emily Brontë)

mine NOUN gold ❑ *Whether both
th'Indias of spice and mine* (*The
Sun Rising* by John Donne)

mire NOUN mud ❑ *Tis my fate to be
always ground into the mire under
the iron heel of oppression* (*The
Adventures of Huckleberry Finn* by
Mark Twain)

miscellany NOUN a miscellany is a
collection of many different kinds
of things ❑ *under that, the miscellany began* (*Treasure Island* by
Robert Louis Stevenson)

mistarshers NOUN mistarshers means
moustache, which is the hair that
grows on a man's upper lip ❑ *when
he put his hand up to his
mistarshers* (*Tess of the
D'Urbervilles* by Thomas Hardy)

morrow NOUN here good-morrow
means tomorrow and a new and
better life ❑ *And now good-morrow
to our waking souls* (*The Good-
Morrow* by John Donne)

mortification NOUN mortification is an
old word for gangrene which is
when part of the body decays or
'dies' because of disease ❑ *Yes, it
was a mortification – that was it*
(*The Adventures of Huckleberry
Finn* by Mark Twain)

mought PARTICIPLE mought is an old
spelling of might ❑ *what you
mought call me? You mought call
me captain* (*Treasure Island* by
Robert Louis Stevenson)

move VERB move me not means do not
make me angry ❑ *Move me not,
Faustus* (*Doctor Faustus 2.1* by
Christopher Marlowe)

muffin-cap NOUN a muffin cap is a flat
cap made from wool ❑ *the old one,
remained stationary in the muffin-
cap and leathers* (*Oliver Twist* by
Charles Dickens)

mulatter NOUN a mulatter was another
word for mulatto, which is a person
with parents who are from different
races ❑ *a mulatter, most as white as*

a white man (*The Adventures of Huckleberry Finn* by Mark Twain)

mummery NOUN mummery is an old word that meant meaningless (or pretentious) ceremony ❑ *When they were all gone, and when Trabb and his men – but not his boy: I looked for him – had crammed their mummery into bags, and were gone too, the house felt wholesomer.* (*Great Expectations* by Charles Dickens)

nap NOUN the nap is the woolly surface on a new item of clothing. Here the surface has been worn away so it looks bare ❑ *like an old hat with the nap rubbed off* (*The Adventures of Huckleberry Finn* by Mark Twain)

natural ■ NOUN a natural is a person born with learning difficulties ❑ *though he had been left to his particular care by their deceased father, who thought him almost a natural.* (*David Copperfield* by Charles Dickens) ■ ADJ natural meant illegitimate ❑ *Harriet Smith was the natural daughter of somebody* (*Emma* by Jane Austen)

navigator NOUN a navigator was originally someone employed to dig canals. It is the origin of the word 'navvy' meaning a labourer ❑ *She ascertained from me in a few words what it was all about, comforted Dora, and gradually convinced her that I was not a labourer – from my manner of stating the case I believe Dora concluded that I was a navigator, and went balancing myself up and down a plank all day with a wheelbarrow – and so brought us together in peace.* (*David Copperfield* by Charles Dickens)

necromancy NOUN necromancy means a kind of magic where the magician speaks to spirits or ghosts to find out what will happen in the future ❑ *He surfeits upon cursed necromancy* (*Doctor Faustus chorus* by Christopher Marlowe)

negus NOUN a negus is a hot drink made from sweetened wine and water ❑ *He sat placidly perusing the newspaper, with his little head on one side, and a glass of warm sherry negus at his elbow.* (*David Copperfield* by Charles Dickens)

nice ADJ discriminating. Able to make good judgements or choices ❑ *consequently a claim to be nice* (*Emma* by Jane Austen)

nigh ADV nigh means near ❑ *He'll never know how nigh he come to getting lynched* (*The Adventures of Huckleberry Finn* by Mark Twain)

nimbleness NOUN nimbleness means being able to move very quickly or skillfully ❑ *and with incredible accuracy and nimbleness* (*Treasure Island* by Robert Louis Stevenson)

noggin NOUN a noggin is a small mug or a wooden cup ❑ *you'll bring me one noggin of rum* (*Treasure Island* by Robert Louis Stevenson)

none ADJ neither ❑ *none can die* (*The Good-Morrow* by John Donne)

notices NOUN observations ❑ *Arch are his notices* (*The Prelude* by William Wordsworth)

occiput NOUN occiput means the back of the head ❑ *saw off the occiput of each couple* (*Gulliver's Travels* by Jonathan Swift)

officiously ADJ kindly ❑ *the governess who attended Glumdalclitch very officiously lifted me up* (*Gulliver's Travels* by Jonathan Swift)

old salt PHRASE old salt is a slang term for an experienced sailor ❑ *a 'true sea-dog', and a 'real old salt'* (*Treasure Island* by Robert Louis Stevenson)

or ere PHRASE before ❑ *or ere the Hall was built* (*The Prelude* by William Wordsworth)

ostler NOUN one who looks after horses at an inn ❑ *The bill paid, and the waiter remembered, and the ostler not forgotten, and the chambermaid taken into consideration* (*Great Expectations* by Charles Dickens)

ostry NOUN an ostry is an old word for a pub or hotel ❑ *lest I send you into the ostry with a vengeance* (*Doctor Faustus 2.2* by Christopher Marlowe)

outrunning the constable PHRASE outrunning the constable meant spending more than you earn ❑ *but I shall by this means be able to check your bills and to pull you up if I find you outrunning the constable.* (*Great Expectations* by Charles Dickens)

over ADJ across ❑ *It is in length six yards, and in the thickest part at least three yards over* (*Gulliver's Travels* by Jonathan Swift)

over the broomstick PHRASE this is a phrase meaning 'getting married without a formal ceremony' ❑ *They both led tramping lives, and this woman in Gerrard-street here, had been married very young, over the broomstick (as we say), to a tramping man, and was a perfect fury in point of jealousy.* (*Great Expectations* by Charles Dickens)

own VERB own means to admit or to acknowledge ❑ *It's my old girl that advises. She has the head. But I never own to it before her. Discipline must be maintained* (*Bleak House* by Charles Dickens)

page NOUN here page means a boy employed to run errands ❑ *not my feigned page* (*On His Mistress* by John Donne)

paid pretty dear PHRASE paid pretty dear means paid a high price or suffered quite a lot ❑ *I paid pretty dear for my monthly fourpenny piece* (*Treasure Island* by Robert Louis Stevenson)

pannikins NOUN pannikins were small tin cups ❑ *of lifting light glasses and cups to his lips, as if they were clumsy pannikins* (*Great Expectations* by Charles Dickens)

pards NOUN pards are leopards ❑ *Not charioted by Bacchus and his pards* (*Ode on a Nightingale* by John Keats)

parlour boarder NOUN a pupil who lived with the family ❑ *and somebody had lately raised her from the condition of scholar to parlour boarder* (*Emma* by Jane Austen)

particular, a London PHRASE London in Victorian times and up to the 1950s was famous for having very dense fog – which was a combination of real fog and the smog of pollution from factories ❑ *This is a London particular . . . A fog, miss'* (*Bleak House* by Charles Dickens)

patten NOUN pattens were wooden soles which were fixed to shoes with straps to protect the shoes in wet weather ❑ *carrying a basket like the Great Seal of England in plaited straw, a pair of pattens, a spare shawl, and an umbrella, though it was a fine bright day* (*Great Expectations* by Charles Dickens)

paviour NOUN a paviour was a labourer who worked on the street pavement ❑ *the paviour his pickaxe* (*Oliver Twist* by Charles Dickens)

peccant ADJ peccant means unhealthy ❑ *other peccant humours* (*Gulliver's Travels* by Jonathan Swift)

penetralium NOUN penetralium is a word used to describe the inner rooms of the house ❑ *and I had no desire to aggravate his impatience previous to inspecting the penetralium* (*Wuthering Heights* by Emily Brontë)

pensive ADV pensive means deep in thought or thinking seriously about something ❑ *and she was leaning pensive on a tomb-stone on her right elbow* (*The Adventures of Huckleberry Finn* by Mark Twain)

penury NOUN penury is the state of being extremely poor ❑ *Distress, if not penury, loomed in the distance* (*Tess of the D'Urbervilles* by Thomas Hardy)

perspective NOUN telescope ❑ *a pocket perspective* (*Gulliver's Travels* by Jonathan Swift)

phaeton NOUN a phaeton was an open carriage for four people ❑ *often* *condescends to drive by my humble abode in her little phaeton and ponies* (*Pride and Prejudice* by Jane Austen)

phantasm NOUN a phantasm is an illusion, something that is not real. It is sometimes used to mean ghost ❑ *Experience had bred no fancies in him that could raise the phantasm of appetite* (*Silas Marner* by George Eliot)

physic NOUN here physic means medicine ❑ *there I studied physic two years and seven months* (*Gulliver's Travels* by Jonathan Swift)

pinioned VERB to pinion is to hold both arms so that a person cannot move them ❑ *But the relentless Ghost pinioned him in both his arms, and forced him to observe what happened next.* (*A Christmas Carol* by Charles Dickens)

piquet NOUN piquet was a popular card game in the C18th ❑ *Mr Hurst and Mr Bingley were at piquet* (*Pride and Prejudice* by Jane Austen)

plaister NOUN a plaister is a piece of cloth on which an apothecary (or pharmacist) would spread ointment. The cloth is then applied to wounds or bruises to treat them ❑ *Then, she gave the knife a final smart wipe on the edge of the plaister, and then sawed a very thick round off the loaf: which she finally, before separating from the loaf, hewed into two halves, of which Joe got one, and I the other.* (*Great Expectations* by Charles Dickens)

plantations NOUN here plantations means colonies, which are countries controlled by a more powerful country ❑ *besides our plantations in America* (*Gulliver's Travels* by Jonathan Swift)

plastic ADV here plastic is an old term meaning shaping or a power that was forming ❑ *A plastic power abode with me* (*The Prelude* by William Wordsworth)

players NOUN actors ❑ *of players which*

upon the world's stage be (*On His Mistress* by John Donne)

plump ADV all at once, suddenly ❑ *But it took a bit of time to get it well round, the change come so uncommon plump, didn't it? (Great Expectations* by Charles Dickens)

plundered VERB to plunder is to rob or steal from ❑ *These crosses stand for the names of ships or towns that they sank or plundered* (*Treasure Island* by Robert Louis Stevenson)

pommel ■ VERB to pommel someone is to hit them repeatedly with your fists ❑ *hug him round the neck, pommel his back, and kick his legs in irrepressible affection!* (*A Christmas Carol* by Charles Dickens) ■ NOUN a pommel is the part of a saddle that rises up at the front ❑ *He had his gun across his pommel* (*The Adventures of Huckleberry Finn* by Mark Twain)

poor's rates NOUN poor's rates were property taxes which were used to support the poor ❑ *"Oh!" replied the undertaker; "why, you know, Mr. Bumble, I pay a good deal towards the poor's rates."* (*Oliver Twist* by Charles Dickens)

popular ADJ popular means ruled by the people, or Republican, rather than ruled by a monarch ❑ *With those of Greece compared and popular Rome* (*The Prelude* by William Wordsworth)

porringer NOUN a porringer is a small bowl ❑ *Of this festive composition each boy had one porringer, and no more* (*Oliver Twist* by Charles Dickens)

postboy NOUN a postboy was the driver of a horse-drawn carriage ❑ *He spoke to a postboy who was dozing under the gateway* (*Oliver Twist* by Charles Dickens)

post-chaise NOUN a fast carriage for two or four passengers ❑ *Looking round, he saw that it was a post-chaise, driven at great speed* (*Oliver Twist* by Charles Dickens)

postern NOUN a small gate usually at the back of a building ❑ *The little servant happening to be entering the fortress with two hot rolls, I passed through the postern and crossed the drawbridge, in her company* (*Great Expectations* by Charles Dickens)

pottle NOUN a pottle was a small basket ❑ *He had a paper-bag under each arm and a pottle of strawberries in one hand . . .* (*Great Expectations* by Charles Dickens)

pounce NOUN pounce is a fine powder used to prevent ink spreading on untreated paper ❑ *in that grim atmosphere of pounce and parchment, red-tape, dusty wafers, ink-jars, brief and draft paper, law reports, writs, declarations, and bills of costs* (*David Copperfield* by Charles Dickens)

pox NOUN pox means sexually transmitted diseases like syphilis ❑ *how the pox in all its consequences and denominations* (*Gulliver's Travels* by Jonathan Swift)

prelibation NOUN prelibation means a foretaste of or an example of something to come ❑ *A prelibation to the mower's scythe* (*The Prelude* by William Wordsworth)

prentice NOUN an apprentice ❑ *and Joe, sitting on an old gun, had told me that when I was 'prentice to him regularly bound, we would have such Larks there!* (*Great Expectations* by Charles Dickens)

presently ADV immediately ❑ *I presently knew what they meant* (*Gulliver's Travels* by Jonathan Swift)

pumpion NOUN pumpkin ❑ *for it was almost as large as a small pumpion* (*Gulliver's Travels* by Jonathan Swift)

punctual ADJ kept in one place ❑ *was not a punctual presence, but a spirit* (*The Prelude* by William Wordsworth)

quadrille ■ NOUN a quadrille is a dance invented in France which is usually performed by four couples ❑ *However, Mr Swiveller had Miss Sophy's hand for the first quadrille (country-dances being low, were utterly proscribed)* (*The Old Curiosity Shop* by Charles Dickens) ■ NOUN quadrille was a card game for four people ❑ *to make up her pool of quadrille in the evening* (*Pride and Prejudice* by Jane Austen)

quality NOUN gentry or upper-class people ❑ *if you are with the quality* (*The Adventures of Huckleberry Finn* by Mark Twain)

quick parts PHRASE quick-witted ❑ *Mr Bennet was so odd a mixture of quick parts* (*Pride and Prejudice* by Jane Austen)

quid NOUN a quid is something chewed or kept in the mouth, like a piece of tobacco ❑ *rolling his quid* (*Treasure Island* by Robert Louis Stevenson)

quit VERB quit means to avenge or to make even ❑ *But Faustus's death shall quit my infamy* (*Doctor Faustus 4.3* by Christopher Marlowe)

rags NOUN divisions ❑ *Nor hours, days, months, which are the rags of time* (*The Sun Rising* by John Donne)

raiment NOUN raiment means clothing ❑ *the mountain shook off turf and flower, had only heath for raiment and crag for gem* (*Jane Eyre* by Charlotte Brontë)

rain cats and dogs PHRASE an expression meaning rain heavily. The origin of the expression is unclear ❑ *But it'll perhaps rain cats and dogs to-morrow* (*Silas Marner* by George Eliot)

raised Cain PHRASE raised Cain means caused a lot of trouble. Cain is a character in the Bible who killed his brother Abel ❑ *and every time he got drunk he raised Cain around town* (*The Adventures of Huckleberry Finn* by Mark Twain)

rambling ADJ rambling means confused and not very clear ❑ *my* *head began to be filled very early with rambling thoughts (Robinson Crusoe by Daniel Defoe)*

raree-show NOUN a raree-show is an old term for a peep-show or a fairground entertainment ❑ *A raree-show is here, with children gathered round (The Prelude by William Wordsworth)*

recusants NOUN people who resisted authority ❑ *hardy recusants (The Prelude by William Wordsworth)*

redounding VERB eddying. An eddy is a movement in water or air which goes round and round instead of flowing in one direction ❑ *mists and steam-like fogs redounding everywhere (The Prelude by William Wordsworth)*

redundant ADJ here redundant means overflowing but Wordsworth also uses it to mean excessively large or too big ❑ *A tempest, a redundant energy (The Prelude by William Wordsworth)*

reflex NOUN reflex is a shortened version of reflexion, which is an alternative spelling of reflection ❑ *To cut across the reflex of a star (The Prelude by William Wordsworth)*

Reformatory NOUN a prison for young offenders/criminals ❑ *Even when I was taken to have a new suit of clothes, the tailor had orders to make them like a kind of Reformatory, and on no account to let me have the free use of my limbs. (Great Expectations by Charles Dickens)*

remorse NOUN pity or compassion ❑ *by that remorse (On His Mistress by John Donne)*

render VERB in this context render means give. ❑ *and Sarah could render no reason that would be sanctioned by the feeling of the community. (Silas Marner by George Eliot)*

repeater NOUN a repeater was a watch that chimed the last hour when a button was pressed – as a result it

was useful in the dark ❑ *And his watch is a gold repeater, and worth a hundred pound if it's worth a penny. (Great Expectations by Charles Dickens)*

repugnance NOUN repugnance means a strong dislike of something or someone ❑ *overcoming a strong repugnance (Treasure Island by Robert Louis Stevenson)*

reverence NOUN reverence means bow. When you bow to someone, you briefly bend your body towards them as a formal way of showing them respect ❑ *made my reverence (Gulliver's Travels by Jonathan Swift)*

reverie NOUN a reverie is a day dream ❑ *I can guess the subject of your reverie (Pride and Prejudice by Jane Austen)*

revival NOUN a religious meeting held in public ❑ *well I'd ben a-running' a little temperance revival thar' bout a week (The Adventures of Huckleberry Finn by Mark Twain)*

revolt VERB revolt means turn back or stop your present course of action and go back to what you were doing before ❑ *Revolt, or I'll in piecemeal tear thy flesh (Doctor Faustus 5.1 by Christopher Marlowe)*

rheumatics/rheumatism NOUN rheumatics [rheumatism] is an illness that makes your joints or muscles stiff and painful ❑ *a new cure for the rheumatics (Treasure Island by Robert Louis Stevenson)*

riddance NOUN riddance is usually used in the form good riddance which you say when you are pleased that something has gone or been left behind ❑ *I'd better go into the house, and die and be a riddance (David Copperfield by Charles Dickens)*

rimy ADJ rimy is an ADJective which means covered in ice or frost ❑ *It was a rimy morning, and very damp (Great Expectations by Charles Dickens)*

riper ADJ riper means more mature or older ❑ *At riper years to Wittenberg he went* (*Doctor Faustus chorus* by Christopher Marlowe)

rubber NOUN a set of games in whist or backgammon ❑ *her father was sure of his rubber* (*Emma* by Jane Austen)

ruffian NOUN a ruffian is a person who behaves violently ❑ *and when the ruffian had told him* (*Treasure Island* by Robert Louis Stevenson)

sadness NOUN sadness is an old term meaning seriousness ❑ *But I prithee tell me, in good sadness* (*Doctor Faustus 2.2* by Christopher Marlowe)

sailed before the mast PHRASE this phrase meant someone who did not look like a sailor ❑ *he had none of the appearance of a man that sailed before the mast* (*Treasure Island* by Robert Louis Stevenson)

scabbard NOUN a scabbard is the covering for a sword or dagger ❑ *Girded round its middle was an antique scabbard; but no sword was in it, and the ancient sheath was eaten up with rust* (*A Christmas Carol* by Charles Dickens)

schooners NOUN A schooner is a fast, medium-sized sailing ship ❑ *if schooners, islands, and maroons* (*Treasure Island* by Robert Louis Stevenson)

science NOUN learning or knowledge ❑ *Even Science, too, at hand* (*The Prelude* by William Wordsworth)

scrouge VERB to scrouge means to squeeze or to crowd ❑ *to scrouge in and get a sight* (*The Adventures of Huckleberry Finn* by Mark Twain)

scrutore NOUN a scrutore, or escritoire, was a writing table ❑ *set me gently on my feet upon the scrutore* (*Gulliver's Travels* by Jonathan Swift)

scutcheon/escutcheon NOUN an escutcheon is a shield with a coat of arms, or the symbols of a family name, engraved on it ❑ *On the*

scutcheon we'll have a bend (*The Adventures of Huckleberry Finn* by Mark Twain)

sea-dog PHRASE sea-dog is a slang term for an experienced sailor or pirate ❑ *a 'true sea-dog', and a 'real old salt,'* (*Treasure Island* by Robert Louis Stevenson)

see the lions PHRASE to see the lions was to go and see the sights of London. Originally the phrase referred to the menagerie in the Tower of London and later in Regent's Park ❑ *We will go and see the lions for an hour or two – it's something to have a fresh fellow like you to show them to, Copperfield* (*David Copperfield* by Charles Dickens)

self-conceit NOUN self-conceit is an old term which means having too high an opinion of oneself, or deceiving yourself ❑ *Till swollen with cunning, of a self-conceit* (*Doctor Faustus chorus* by Christopher Marlowe)

seneschal NOUN a steward ❑ *where a grey-headed seneschal sings a funny chorus with a funnier body of vassals* (*Oliver Twist* by Charles Dickens)

sensible ADJ if you were sensible of something you are aware or conscious of something ❑ *If my children are silly I must hope to be always sensible of it* (*Pride and Prejudice* by Jane Austen)

sessions NOUN court cases were heard at specific times of the year called sessions ❑ *He lay in prison very ill, during the whole interval between his committal for trial, and the coming round of the Sessions.* (*Great Expectations* by Charles Dickens)

shabby ADJ shabby places look old and in bad condition ❑ *a little bit of a shabby village named Pikesville* (*The Adventures of Huckleberry Finn* by Mark Twain)

shay-cart NOUN a shay-cart was a small cart drawn by one horse ❑ *"I were at the Bargemen t'other night, Pip;"*

whenever he subsided into affection, he called me Pip, and whenever he relapsed into politeness he called me Sir; "when there come up in his shay-cart Pumblechook." (*Great Expectations* by Charles Dickens)

shilling NOUN a shilling is an old unit of currency. There were twenty shillings in every British pound ❑ *"Ten shillings too much," said the gentleman in the white waistcoat.* (*Oliver Twist* by Charles Dickens)

shines NOUN tricks or games ❑ *well, it would make a cow laugh to see the shines that old idiot cut* (*The Adventures of Huckleberry Finn* by Mark Twain)

shirking VERB shirking means not doing what you are meant to be doing, or evading your duties ❑ *some of you shirking lubbers* (*Treasure Island* by Robert Louis Stevenson)

shiver my timbers PHRASE shiver my timbers is an expression which was used by sailors and pirates to express surprise ❑ *why, shiver my timbers, if I hadn't forgotten my score!* (*Treasure Island* by Robert Louis Stevenson)

shoe-roses NOUN shoe-roses were roses made from ribbons which were stuck on to shoes as decoration ❑ *the very shoe-roses for Netherfield were got by proxy* (*Pride and Prejudice* by Jane Austen)

singular ADJ singular means very great and remarkable or strange ❑ *"Singular dream," he says* (*The Adventures of Huckleberry Finn* by Mark Twain)

sire NOUN sire is an old word which means lord or master or elder ❑ *She also defied her sire* (*Little Women* by Louisa May Alcott)

sixpence NOUN a sixpence was half of a shilling ❑ *if she had only a shilling in the world, she would be very likely to give away sixpence of it* (*Emma* by Jane Austen)

slavey NOUN the word slavey was used when there was only one servant in a house or boarding-house – so she had to perform all the duties of a larger staff ❑ *Two distinct knocks, sir, will produce the slavey at any time* (*The Old Curiosity Shop* by Charles Dickens)

slender ADJ weak ❑ *In slender accents of sweet verse* (*The Prelude* by William Wordsworth)

slop-shops NOUN slop-shops were shops where cheap ready-made clothes were sold. They mainly sold clothes to sailors ❑ *Accordingly, I took the jacket off, that I might learn to do without it; and carrying it under my arm, began a tour of inspection of the various slop-shops.* (*David Copperfield* by Charles Dickens)

sluggard NOUN a lazy person ❑ *"Stand up and repeat 'Tis the voice of the sluggard,'" said the Gryphon.* (*Alice's Adventures in Wonderland* by Lewis Carroll)

smallpox NOUN smallpox is a serious infectious disease ❑ *by telling the men we had smallpox aboard* (*The Adventures of Huckleberry Finn* by Mark Twain)

smalls NOUN smalls are short trousers ❑ *It is difficult for a large-headed, small-eyed youth, of lumbering make and heavy countenance, to look dignified under any circumstances; but it is more especially so, when superadded to these personal attractions are a red nose and yellow smalls* (*Oliver Twist* by Charles Dickens)

sneeze-box NOUN a box for snuff was called a sneeze-box because sniffing snuff makes the user sneeze ❑ *To think of Jack Dawkins — lummy Jack — the Dodger — the Artful Dodger — going abroad for a common twopenny-halfpenny sneeze-box!* (*Oliver Twist* by Charles Dickens)

snorted VERB slept ❑ *Or snorted we in the Seven Sleepers' den?* (*The Good-Morrow* by John Donne)

snuff NOUN snuff is tobacco in powder form which is taken by sniffing ❑

as he thrust his thumb and fore-finger into the proffered snuff-box of the undertaker: which was an ingenious little model of a patent coffin. (*Oliver Twist* by Charles Dickens)

soliloquized VERB to soliloquize is when an actor in a play speaks to himself or herself rather than to another actor ❑ *"A new servitude! There is something in that," I soliloquized (mentally, be it understood; I did not talk aloud)* (*Jane Eyre* by Charlotte Brontë)

sough NOUN a sough is a drain or a ditch ❑ *as you may have noticed the sough that runs from the marshes* (*Wuthering Heights* by Emily Brontë)

spirits NOUN a spirit is the nonphysical part of a person which is believed to remain alive after their death ❑ *that I might raise up spirits when I please* (*Doctor Faustus 1.5* by Christopher Marlowe)

spleen ◼ NOUN here spleen means a type of sadness or depression which was thought to only affect the wealthy ❑ *yet here I could plainly discover the true seeds of spleen* (*Gulliver's Travels* by Jonathan Swift) ◼ NOUN irritability and low spirits ❑ *Adieu to disappointment and spleen* (*Pride and Prejudice* by Jane Austen)

spondulicks NOUN spondulicks is a slang word which means money ❑ *not for all his spondulicks and as much more on top of it* (*The Adventures of Huckleberry Finn* by Mark Twain)

stalled of VERB to be stalled of something is to be bored with it ❑ *I'm stalled of doing naught* (*Wuthering Heights* by Emily Brontë)

stanchion NOUN a stanchion is a pole or bar that stands upright and is used as a buidling support ❑ *and slid down a stanchion* (*The Adventures of Huckleberry Finn* by Mark Twain)

stang NOUN stang is another word for pole which was an old measurement ❑ *These fields were intermingled with woods of half a stang* (*Gulliver's Travels* by Jonathan Swift)

starlings NOUN a starling is a wall built around the pillars that support a bridge to protect the pillars ❑ *There were states of the tide when, having been down the river, I could not get back through the eddy-chafed arches and starlings of old London Bridge* (*Great Expectations* by Charles Dickens)

startings NOUN twitching or night-time movements of the body ❑ *with midnight's startings* (*On His Mistress* by John Donne)

stomacher NOUN a panel at the front of a dress ❑ *but send her aunt the pattern of a stomacher* (*Emma* by Jane Austen)

stoop VERB swoop ❑ *Once a kite hovering over the garden made a swoop at me* (*Gulliver's Travels* by Jonathan Swift)

succedaneum NOUN a succedaneum is a substitute ❑ *But as a succedaneum* (*The Prelude* by William Wordsworth)

suet NOUN a hard animal fat used in cooking ❑ *and your jaws are too weak For anything tougher than suet* (*Alice's Adventures in Wonderland* by Lewis Carroll)

sultry ADJ sultry weather is hot and damp. Here sultry means unpleasant or risky ❑ *for it was getting pretty sultry for us* (*The Adventures of Huckleberry Finn* by Mark Twain)

summerset NOUN summerset is an old spelling of somersault. If someone does a somersault, they turn over completely in the air ❑ *I have seen him do the summerset* (*Gulliver's Travels* by Jonathan Swift)

supper NOUN supper was a light meal taken late in the evening. The main meal was dinner which was eaten at four or five in the afternoon ❑ *and the supper table was all set out* (*Emma* by Jane Austen)

surfeits VERB to surfeit in something is to have far too much of it, or to overindulge in it to an unhealthy degree ❑ *He surfeits upon cursed necromancy* (*Doctor Faustus chorus* by Christopher Marlowe)

surtout NOUN a surtout is a long close-fitting overcoat ❑ *He wore a long black surtout reaching nearly to his ankles* (*The Old Curiosity Shop* by Charles Dickens)

swath NOUN swath is the width of corn cut by a scythe ❑ *while thy hook Spares the next swath* (*Ode to Autumn* by John Keats)

sylvan ADJ sylvan means belonging to the woods ❑ *Sylvan historian* (*Ode on a Grecian Urn* by John Keats)

taction NOUN taction means touch. This means that the people had to be touched on the mouth or the ears to get their attention ❑ *without being roused by some external taction upon the organs of speech and hearing* (*Gulliver's Travels* by Jonathan Swift)

Tag and Rag and Bobtail PHRASE the riff-raff, or lower classes. Used in an insulting way ❑ *"No," said he; "not till it got about that there was no protection on the premises, and it come to be considered dangerous, with convicts and Tag and Rag and Bobtail going up and down."* (*Great Expectations* by Charles Dickens)

tallow NOUN tallow is hard animal fat that is used to make candles and soap ❑ *and a lot of tallow candles* (*The Adventures of Huckleberry Finn* by Mark Twain)

tan VERB to tan means to beat or whip ❑ *and if I catch you about that school I'll tan you good* (*The Adventures of Huckleberry Finn* by Mark Twain)

tanyard NOUN the tanyard is part of a tannery, which is a place where leather is made from animal skins ❑ *hid in the old tanyard* (*The Adventures of Huckleberry Finn* by Mark Twain)

tarry ADJ tarry means the colour of tar or black ❑ *his tarry pig-tail* (*Treasure Island* by Robert Louis Stevenson)

thereof PHRASE from there ❑ *By all desires which thereof did ensue* (*On His Mistress* by John Donne)

thick with, be PHRASE if you are 'thick with someone' you are very close, sharing secrets – it is often used to describe people who are planning something secret ❑ *Hasn't he been thick with Mr Heathcliff lately?* (*Wuthering Heights* by Emily Brontë)

thimble NOUN a thimble is a small cover used to protect the finger while sewing ❑ *The paper had been sealed in several places by a thimble* (*Treasure Island* by Robert Louis Stevenson)

thirtover ADJ thirtover is an old word which means obstinate or that someone is very determined to do want they want and can not be persuaded to do something in another way ❑ *I have been living on in a thirtover, lackadaisical way* (*Tess of the D'Urbervilles* by Thomas Hardy)

timbrel NOUN timbrel is a tambourine ❑ *What pipes and timbrels?* (*Ode on a Grecian Urn* by John Keats)

tin NOUN tin is slang for money/cash ❑ *Then the plain question is, an't it a pity that this state of things should continue, and how much better would it be for the old gentleman to hand over a reasonable amount of tin, and make it all right and comfortable* (*The Old Curiosity Shop* by Charles Dickens)

tincture NOUN a tincture is a medicine made with alcohol and a small amount of a drug ❑ *with ink composed of a cephalic tincture* (*Gulliver's Travels* by Jonathan Swift)

tithe NOUN a tithe is a tax paid to the church ❑ *and held farms which, speaking from a spiritual point of view, paid highly-desirable tithes* (*Silas Marner* by George Eliot)

towardly ADJ a towardly child is dutiful or obedient ❑ *and a towardly child* (*Gulliver's Travels* by Jonathan Swift)

toys NOUN trifles are things which are considered to have little importance, value, or significance ❑ *purchase my life from them by some bracelets, glass rings, and other toys* (*Gulliver's Travels* by Jonathan Swift)

tract NOUN a tract is a religious pamphlet or leaflet ❑ *and Joe Harper got a hymn-book and a tract* (*The Adventures of Huckleberry Finn* by Mark Twain)

train-oil NOUN train-oil is oil from whale blubber ❑ *The train-oil and gunpowder were shoved out of sight in a minute* (*Wuthering Heights* by Emily Brontë)

tribulation NOUN tribulation means the suffering or difficulty you experience in a particular situation ❑ *Amy was learning this distinction through much tribulation* (*Little Women* by Louisa May Alcott)

trivet NOUN a trivet is a three-legged stand for resting a pot or kettle ❑ *a pocket-knife in his right; and a pewter pot on the trivet* (*Oliver Twist* by Charles Dickens)

trot line NOUN a trot line is a fishing line to which a row of smaller fishing lines are attached ❑ *when he got along I was hard at it taking up a trot line* (*The Adventures of Huckleberry Finn* by Mark Twain)

troth NOUN oath or pledge ❑ *I wonder, by my troth* (*The Good-Morrow* by John Donne)

truckle NOUN a truckle bedstead is a bed that is on wheels and can be slid under another bed to save space ❑ *It rose under my hand, and the door yielded. Looking in, I saw a lighted candle on a table, a bench, and a mattress on a truckle bedstead.* (*Great Expectations* by Charles Dickens)

trump NOUN a trump is a good, reliable person wo can be trusted ❑ *This lad Hawkins is a trump, I perceive* (*Treasure Island* by Robert Louis Stevenson)

tucker NOUN a tucker is a frilly lace collar which is worn around the neck ❑ *Whereat Scrooge's niece's sister⁻the plump one with the lace tucker: not the one with the roses⁻blushed.* (*A Christmas Carol* by Charles Dickens)

tureen NOUN a large bowl with a lid from which soup or vegetables are served ❑ *Waiting in a hot tureen!* (*Alice's Adventures in Wonderland* by Lewis Carroll)

turnkey NOUN a prison officer; jailer ❑ *As we came out of the prison through the lodge, I found that the great importance of my guardian was appreciated by the turnkeys, no less than by those whom they held in charge.* (*Great Expectations* by Charles Dickens)

turnpike NOUN the upkeep of many roads of the time was paid for by tolls (fees) collected at posts along the road. There was a gate to prevent people travelling further along the road until the toll had been paid. ❑ *Traddles, whom I have taken up by appointment at the turnpike, presents a dazzling combination of cream colour and light blue; and both he and Mr. Dick have a general effect about them of being all gloves.* (*David Copperfield* by Charles Dickens)

twas PHRASE it was ❑ *twas but a dream of thee* (*The Good-Morrow* by John Donne)

tyrannized VERB tyrannized means bullied or forced to do things against their will ❑ *for people would soon cease coming there to be tyrannized over and put down* (*Treasure Island* by Robert Louis Stevenson)

'un NOUN 'un is a slang term for one – usually used to refer to a person ❑ *She's been thinking the old 'un* (*David Copperfield* by Charles Dickens)

undistinguished ADJ undiscriminating or incapable of making a distinction between good and bad things ❑ *their undistinguished appetite to devour everything* (*Gulliver's Travels* by Jonathan Swift)

use NOUN habit ❑ *Though use make you apt to kill me* (*The Flea* by John Donne)

vacant ADJ vacant usually means empty, but here Wordsworth uses it to mean carefree ❑ *To vacant musing, unreproved neglect* (*The Prelude* by William Wordsworth)

valetudinarian NOUN one too concerned with his or her own health. ❑ *for having been a valetudinarian all his life* (*Emma* by Jane Austen)

vamp VERB vamp means to walk or tramp to somewhere ❑ *Well, vamp on to Marlott, will 'ee* (*Tess of the D'Urbervilles* by Thomas Hardy)

vapours NOUN the vapours is an old term which means unpleasant and strange thoughts, which make the person feel nervous and unhappy ❑ *and my head was full of vapours* (*Robinson Crusoe* by Daniel Defoe)

vegetables NOUN here vegetables means plants ❑ *the other vegetables are in the same proportion* (*Gulliver's Travels* by Jonathan Swift)

venturesome ADJ if you are venturesome you are willing to take risks ❑ *he must be either hopelessly stupid or a venturesome fool* (*Wuthering Heights* by Emily Brontë)

verily ADJ verily means really or truly ❑ *though I believe verily* (*Robinson Crusoe* by Daniel Defoe)

vicinage NOUN vicinage is an area or the residents of an area ❑ *and to his thought the whole vicinage was haunted by her.* (*Silas Marner* by George Eliot)

victuals NOUN victuals means food ❑ *grumble a little over the victuals* (*The Adventures of Huckleberry Finn* by Mark Twain)

vintage NOUN vintage in this context means wine ❑ *Oh, for a draught of*

vintage! (*Ode on a Nightingale* by John Keats)

virtual ADJ here virtual means powerful or strong ❑ *had virtual faith* (*The Prelude* by William Wordsworth)

vittles NOUN vittles is a slang word which means food ❑ *There never was such a woman for givin' away vittles and drink* (*Little Women* by Louisa May Alcott)

voided straight PHRASE voided straight is an old expression which means emptied immediately ❑ *see the rooms be voided straight* (*Doctor Faustus 4.1* by Christopher Marlowe)

wainscot NOUN wainscot is wood panel lining in a room so wainscoted means a room lined with wooden panels ❑ *in the dark wainscoted parlor* (*Silas Marner* by George Eliot)

walking the plank PHRASE walking the plank was a punishment in which a prisoner would be made to walk along a plank on the side of the ship and fall into the sea, where they would be abandoned ❑ *about hanging, and walking the plank* (*Treasure Island* by Robert Louis Stevenson)

want VERB want means to be lacking or short of ❑ *The next thing wanted was to get the picture framed* (*Emma* by Jane Austen)

wanting ADJ wanting means lacking or missing ❑ *wanting two fingers of the left hand* (*Treasure Island* by Robert Louis Stevenson)

wanting, I was not PHRASE I was not wanting means I did not fail ❑ *I was not wanting to lay a foundation of religious knowledge in his mind* (*Robinson Crusoe* by Daniel Defoe)

ward NOUN a ward is, usually, a child who has been put under the protection of the court or a guardian for his or her protection ❑ *I call the Wards in Jarndyce. The* are caged up with all the others. (*Bleak House* by Charles Dickens)

waylay VERB to waylay someone is to lie in wait for them or to intercept them ❑ *I must go up the road and waylay him* (*The Adventures of Huckleberry Finn* by Mark Twain)

weazen NOUN weazen is a slang word for throat. It actually means shrivelled ❑ *You with a uncle too! Why, I knowed you at Gargery's when you was so small a wolf that I could have took your weazen betwixt this finger and thumb and chucked you away dead* (*Great Expectations* by Charles Dickens)

wery ◼ ADV very ❑ *Be wery careful o' vidders all your life* (*Pickwick Papers* by Charles Dickens) ◼ *See* wibrated

wherry NOUN wherry is a small swift rowing boat for one person ❑ *It was flood tide when Daniel Quilp sat himself down in the wherry to cross to the opposite shore.* (*The Old Curiosity Shop* by Charles Dickens)

whether PREP whether means which of the two in this example ❑ *we came in full view of a great island or continent (for we knew not whether)* (*Gulliver's Travels* by Jonathan Swift)

whetstone NOUN a whetstone is a stone used to sharpen knives and other tools ❑ *I dropped pap's whetstone there too* (*The Adventures of Huckleberry Finn* by Mark Twain)

wibrated VERB in Dickens's use of the English language 'w' often replaces 'v' when he is reporting speech. So here 'wibrated' means 'vibrated'. In Pickwick Papers a judge asks Sam Weller (who constantly confuses the two letters) 'Do you spell it with a 'v' or a 'w'?' to which Weller replies 'That depends upon the taste and fancy of the speller, my Lord' ❑ *There are strings . . . in the human heart that had better not be wibrated'* (*Barnaby Rudge* by Charles Dickens)

wicket NOUN a wicket is a little door in a larger entrance ❑ *Having rested here, for a minute or so, to collect a good burst of sobs and an imposing show of tears and terror, he knocked loudly at the wicket;* (*Oliver Twist* by Charles Dickens)

without CONJ without means unless ❑ *You don't know about me, without you have read a book by the name of The Adventures of Tom Sawyer* (*The Adventures of Huckleberry Finn* by Mark Twain)

wittles ◼ NOUN vittles is a slang word which means food ❑ *I live on broken wittles – and I sleep on the coals* (*David Copperfield* by Charles Dickens) ◼ *See* wibrated

woo VERB courts or forms a proper relationship with ❑ *before it woo* (*The Flea* by John Donne)

words, to have PHRASE if you have words with someone you have a disagreement or an argument ❑ *I do not want to have words with a young thing like you.* (*Black Beauty* by Emily Brontë)

workhouse NOUN workhouses were places where the homeless were given food and a place to live in return for doing very hard work ❑ *And the Union workhouses? demanded Scrooge. Are they still in operation?* (*A Christmas Carol* by Charles Dickens)

yawl NOUN a yawl is a small boat kept on a bigger boat for short trips. Yawl is also the name for a small fishing boat ❑ *She sent out her yawl, and we went aboard* (*The Adventures of Huckleberry Finn* by Mark Twain)

yeomanry NOUN the yeomanry was a collective term for the middle classes involved in agriculture ❑ *The yeomanry are precisely the order of people with whom I feel I can have nothing to do* (*Emma* by Jane Austen)

yonder ADV yonder means over there ❑ *all in the same second we seem to hear low voices in yonder!* (*The Adventures of Huckleberry Finn* by Mark Twain)